HOW TO SUCCEED IN COLLEGE

HOW TO SUCCEED IN COLLEGE

Barbara Mayer

VGM Career Horizons
a division of *NTC Publishing Group*
Lincolnwood, Illinois USA

Library of Congress Cataloging-in-Publication Data

Mayer, Barbara.
   How to succeed in college / by Barbara Mayer.—2nd ed.

      p.   cm.
   Rev. ed. of: The college survival guide. c1981.
   ISBN 0-8442-4166-0
   1. College student orientation—United States—Handbooks, manuals,
etc. I. Mayer, Barbara. College survival guide. II. Title.
LB2343.32.M39 1992
378.1′98—dc20   92-15710
                                                   CIP

Published by VGM Career Horizons, a division of NTC Publishing Group.
© 1993 by NTC Publishing Group, 4255 West Touhy Avenue,
Lincolnwood (Chicago), Illinois 60646-1975 U.S.A.

2 3 4 5 6 7 8 9 0 VP 9 8 7 6 5 4 3 2 1

Dedication *For Bill—For John*
Our best knowledge came from Albi's love

Contents

THE MOST IMPORTANT SUBJECT— YOU!

Part I

Success

Seek Your Own Level of Excellence

The best way to succeed in college is the best way to succeed in many aspects of life—break through the stereotypes and approach life with realistic honesty. Live beyond the stereotypes and work toward your own level of personal excellence.

Ask anyone about college students today and he or she will rattle off a list of stereotypes. First there are those students who are simply continuing adolescence, no pressure, lots of fun, just four more years of a good time—with no parents or adults around to make things difficult. These people look for the big party schools or make anyplace they are a party as much as they can. They basically aren't interested in learning any great skills or concepts; they want to have a good time. Meeting a possible marriage partner would be icing on the cake.

The second type of student knows a college degree is essential for getting a meaningful job in today's society. This student, however, is certain he or she will fall into a prestigious, $30,000-a-year job right after graduation, and this will all happen without competing for that job or having a well-rounded knowledge of what is necessary to do it.

But there is a third type of person on college campuses today. These individuals really want to learn. They are aware of the ever-tightening job market and the need for strong skills and wide experience and knowledge. These people are neither eggheads nor sticks-in-the-mud. They have a good time—at times—yet keep a strong perspective on the big picture and why all that money is being spent for a college degree. Sadly, though, these types of people are never in the majority on any college campus.

The Right Approach

Whether you are approaching the college scene for the first time or are well-involved in your college education already, you may need to face some hard facts. College, and all it involves, is not an extension of adolescence. Your college years are not meant to be a continuance of childhood or an expensive excuse for keeping reality off the doorstep.

The signs are all around us. More and more people seeking any kind of job—let alone a meaningful and successful career in a demanding job market—know that only the skilled and highly motivated person will succeed in the adult world. America now competes on a new and broader scale with highly advanced financial, creative, business, and production methods not only from industrialized nations in Europe and Asia, but also from many other developing countries as well.

Sound a bit scary? It shouldn't be. With the world changing, however, this may not be the time to view college as some movies have portrayed it. College is neither an "animal house" nor a perpetual party scene. No matter how many people around you still believe in that myth and act accordingly, this book is about *your* success. If others set themselves on the road to failure and delusion, let them be. You are worth more. If you're still reading, you know you are worth more. College can be a good time and a powerful springboard into that future which waits for you. It can be one of the most terrific times of your life—once you understand what it's all about, and how to make it work for you.

What is the key to success in your college years? Simple. Live beyond everyone else's stereotypes. Seek your own level of excellence—in motivation, career, achievement, knowledge, and friends. Most of all, seek a level of excellence in your own personal development.

A Time for Beginning Again

These years in college are supposed to be a challenge to you. The challenge, however, is not whether you will survive the physical demands of school or the pressures others put on you. Instead, the challenge involves how well you use these years to your best advantage and find the successes that mean the most to you.

Any college or university is geared to teach many things, yet there are no classes or textbooks that can give you real knowledge of the most important thing you need to learn about: yourself. If you make it through to graduation, your diploma will say you've achieved a certain amount of skill in the arts, in business, or in some particular field, yet it is you who matters most. One of the healthiest things any graduate from college should be able to say is, "I did get a degree in that particular subject, but I also feel I earned a degree in myself."

Egotistical? The words of a real snob? Absolutely not!

Your professors, friends, classmates, and family are all concerned about your success in different aspects of life. No one, however, really cares about you as much as you do, or as you should. Because of this, before you tackle any of the individual problems or pressures the college scene can throw at you, the most basic things you'll have to understand are who you are, what you are, and where you are going. You may need to go back to a very basic drawing board.

Do you know what college is really all about? There are a lot of people who say a college degree is necessary for success. One quick look around, though, will show you that's not always true. That diploma, the goal of these four years, isn't any great insurance that you will have a higher income than someone who has never earned a college degree. Decide in your own mind why college is necessary to the goals you have set. If the goals aren't that clear yet, it may be time to set them down on paper. Your own words staring back at you will give you a big dose of reality. Are you goal-oriented and self-motivated, or are you going through the motions because you feel it's expected of you? Are you keeping Mom and Dad happy, or are you working toward your own long-term happiness?

What about people? Are you still secure in your own little shell, comfortable with just a few close friends and a bit nervous about going out and meeting the rest of the world? Are you learning for yourself, or just because of others' expectations of you? Is shooting for an *A* in a certain class your goal? Do you want that grade because it's important to you and your understanding of a particular subject, or are you simply trying to please, impress, or compete with someone else?

Do you consider yourself independent enough to think your own thoughts and make your own decisions, or are you the typical follower? Do you feel you have the ability to lead, at least once in a while, or are you going to be— through college and for the rest of your life—someone who waits for others to make the first move?

Looking at the total college scene can be confusing. The one consistent thing you have going for yourself as you tackle any problem or situation is yourself! Learn about that complicated but wonderful person in the mirror, and your college years as well as your life will be full of the success you seek.

Me: 101   Forget the rest of your schedule for a while, and how many credits you're trying to achieve in any semester. The most important thing you'll study any year of college will be in that uniquely complex subject—yourself. In fact, you may not go on for future degrees, but by the time it's all over, you should feel you have attained a doctorate in the one critical aspect of your life—self-knowledge.

How much are you willing to give up your own preferences for popularity or success? Once you decide what is really important in your life, a lot of these decisions and the pressure you feel from teachers, groups, and even friends and family become easier to handle.

What do you want from college? There are people who rub elbows with you every day, who sit in your classes, and who may be very much a part of your life. They may not expect more out of school than a good time and a possible marriage partner. How serious are you about a career, anyway?

Do you have specific goals or job possibilities? Or are you still trying to find where your true talents and potentials lie? If so, are you willing to work hard enough to find out? The sooner you zero in on some goals, the sooner all the pressure and hard work of college will become easier. The longer you drift through school without setting any specific goal, the harder it will be to keep up your interest in a boring class or your enthusiasm to continue doing papers for some professor who seems satisfied only with unreal amounts of outside reading and research.

Take a look in the mirror. Ask yourself why you really are in school. Where do you, in all honesty, see it all going?

If you can come up with even partial answers, you are

well on the way. You can achieve not only success the world can measure, but also the knowledge that you as a person are becoming someone of quality.

Keeping the Options Open

One thing you can be sure of in these college years, and through the rest of your life, is that things will change. By choosing certain classes, friends, and even your school itself, you have already made some important decisions. You may feel you have an idea of where it's all going, and at this point, that's great!

Just remember that the future is an unwritten page. Do yourself a favor and make sure you give yourself the greatest number of alternatives as you move on through school. Develop as many skills as you can; diplomas don't get jobs, capable people do!

As you understand more about yourself, try to understand more about that possible career you are aiming toward. Keep your options open. Give yourself a few escape routes by your choice of classes, especially electives, and don't be afraid to explore new areas of interest where you may have talent that, at this point may still be unknown to you.

You'll read about grades later. At the beginning of any assessment of college, however, it might be good to ask yourself whether you really want to learn or just receive good grades. There are ways to "ace" any class if you really just want that *A*. If you expect to learn something, however, it may take a bit more effort on your part and a little more investigation of a particular subject than even your professors or teaching assistants demand. True learning is measured by what has gotten into your thinking and your life, not by what you manage to answer correctly on a computer answer sheet.

Only you will determine how much you learn in college because only you know your real desires, interests, and potential. You know when you've done your best, and you know when you're just getting by, no matter what others think of your performance. They may be impressed by what you've done. Only you know what could have been better and what you still have not done.

If you can start believing in yourself, you will have just passed your most important course in college. The class is called *Me: 101*.

Self-Check

1. Explain to your own satisfaction your real reasons for attending college.

   _____

   _____

2. What may be keeping you from having more confidence in yourself as a person?

   _____

   _____

3. Now that you are in college, have you begun to see any value to all its demands?

   _____

   How much of what you are doing is done because you think it is really right for you?

   _____

   What are other motives? _____

4. On a scale of 1–10, 10 being the highest, how do you rate your ability to free yourself from pressures others put on you?

   _____

   How do you rate yourself as a leader, at least in your own life?

   _____

   _____

5. Rate your ability to be independent. _____

   Do you feel capable of outlining your own goals and making your own decisions?

   _____

   What are some proofs of this? _____

   _____

6. What are some concrete ways you can start asserting yourself more without alienating others?

_____

_____

_____

Attitude

2

It's All in Your Head

Tackling any situation life can throw at you will always call into play one of the most critical aspects of your individuality—your attitude, both toward the general situation and toward all its specific aspects.

You've come a long way since your parents or kindergarten teacher may have remarked, "I don't like your attitude." Your attitude toward yourself and life has gone through many refinements since your early years. College, however, demands another change in attitude, and this one is crucial. While others around you may choose to waste their college years with alcohol, drugs, or laziness, your seriousness of attitude becomes extremely critical. The tone you set in college is the tone you will most probably take with you out into the adult world.

There must come a time when you get serious about it all. That's when you leave "the kid" behind. While many wonderful childlike attributes remain with us through all our lives, it is the dependent attitude of childhood that has no place in the adult world. Are you a self-starter? What does it take to get you going? If it is anything outside of you, you're still very much "the kid."

Get Serious!
There will be no real success in college or anywhere else in your world until you learn to understand your attitude and make yourself its master. The work world has become much more demanding lately. Competition is much stronger for jobs. The college diploma isn't always enough. Personnel directors are looking for more maturity and a sense of purpose. They are experts at spotting the four-year party animal who suddenly gets a power tie (or power high heels) and a new suit and then tries to act like he or she can be useful to the real world.

Along with doing your textbook and reading assignments, work to develop an attitude of openness and a willingness to work. A healthy, giving, and well-directed attitude is important for those who will succeed. So is an honest work ethic with specific skills to offer any future employer.

Respect Yourself
You would have to be either a saint or an unrealistically naive person to expect everyone to like your attitude all the time. There will be days when pressures get to you or you just can't work up the energy to be aware of others or be concerned about what is important to them. There will be times when others bore you, and you will want to move ahead into projects or ideas that seem more challenging or more compatible with your own preferences.

Most people are realistic and know you won't always be at your best. They know you'll have your good days and bad days, and they'll try to understand. The people who really care about you will try, and these are the people who matter most. (Likewise, be prepared to cut them some slack on *their* off days.)

What others think of your attitude will, of course, affect the way they treat you. It will either open a few doors for you or slam them in your face. You may have the tendency to be very aggressive, for example, and that often scares people. No one likes to be assaulted by another's overbearing personality.

On the other hand, you may be timid, never asserting yourself, never quite confident enough to let others know how you feel. In cases like this, most people will tend to simply ignore you as they move ahead with their own plans and ideas. What can you do about it?

Don't Mimic a Cynic!

There's a lot of cynicism in the world today, and, as isolated as the college campus may be, it hasn't been so separated from the rest of society that it has managed to keep that cynicism out. There are too many young people who, looking at the world today, see nothing but gloom and doom. They look to the future and see no hope. Grim? Yes. Realistic? Never!

There are many excuses for being cynical about the future. Economic hard times and the bleak job picture have left many young people nervous about their possibilities of success. Drugs remain a problem in our society, and with the civil rights movement of the sixties receding from memory, racism and intolerance again are growing with the upsurge in various hate groups and self-serving sects. This world, the one that waits for you, has some real problems, and you'll have to decide at this point of your life if you're going to help solve them, or just create more troubles that others will have to deal with. It's an easy choice, really. You want what is best for you—and your best, in turn, will be what is best for society. You must face society's ills with courage and some positive, creative thinking. The world is not going to end, and there are still many good things to enjoy, to feel, and to be part of. How much you let the problems of society depress you will affect your college years, as well as the rest of your life.

The true cynic is an absolutely miserable human being. He or she is easily recognized by a superior attitude and a snobbish toleration of most things and people. Nothing for this person, is ever really good or right. There are always too many negative components in any situation to make it acceptable. The cynic looks around and finds nothing that can escape his or her criticism.

You may know some people like this; they're easy to spot because of their bitterness and negative attitudes. And unless they hold some position of power, or force themselves on others, they are often very lonely people. It's no wonder! Who in his or her right mind would choose to stay near a prophet of bitterness and doom?

The Easy Choice

Cynicism is a lot like yawning or the flu. It's very contagious! You may not see those negative feelings as they start creeping into your thinking; they can be very subtle at first. There may come a time, however, when you find yourself becoming a little more judgmental, a bit more critical, a little less optimistic and genuinely excited about life's possibilities. These are the first warning signs of chronic cynicism. If you find them creeping into your life and into your words, you may need a strong dose of good old positive mental attitude—immediately!

Do yourself and the world another favor. When you feel something is not as good as you would like it to be, or when someone else doesn't quite measure up to your standards, think a while before you criticize. Most people are very sensitive, and negative judgments from others only make them withdraw further into their shells. That, by the way, is the reason most young people don't talk enough or actively take control of situations. They've already met with so much negativism, criticism, and cynicism that they don't want to invite any more.

That's the way it is, but it's not the way it has to be. Be one of the growing minority who starts seeing the good in things, and who sees the possibilities for better things to come. If cynicism can be contagious, a positive attitude can be, too. A realistic but cheerful approach to your own life will make you a more popular and more enjoyable person. It also will make you a positive influence in an increasingly cynical world. People will come to respect you and admire you more because you have the courage to be happy.

It does take personal courage to stay in a happy frame of mind—courage and energy. Negativism and unhappiness come from a lack of psychological energy. When one is too tired to try, he or she easily becomes depressed or critical. Reach down and tap some of that energy hiding inside. Use it to be more positive and caring, and you'll find realistic happiness growing in your own life.

Tear Down Some Walls

If you really intend to succeed in college, and the rest of life, sooner or later you'll have to begin to deal with all the diversity you're meeting now. There are new ideas bombarding you from all sides. You are meeting different people from cultures and backgrounds strange to you. There are, possibly, a few rugged individuals who are trying to convert you to one opinion or another. With the growing number of adults going back to college for their degrees or for retraining, you as a person in your early 20s may find yourself dealing with older people in your classes. How do you treat them? Do you make them feel comfortable, or do you ignore them, angry because they have invaded your world?

Open-mindedness is something most people feel they possess. Being truly open to new possibilities, however, demands not only your confidence and ability to handle what's up ahead, but also a basic faith in yourself. You have to believe you possess the ability to change directions and go on. If college is doing anything for you right now, it should be pushing back the walls of inexperience that may have kept your life narrow and limited.

Allow those walls to be pushed far back, not through tension and pressure, but with an openness and willingness to see what's out there. Be ready to experience much, and then to sift through it gradually, finding the things you choose to make part of your life. Also, decide where you are wasting your time, which people don't really matter in a positive way, and how your future is shaping up.

All those new people on the college scene can do one of two things. They can force you back into your shell and make you more determined than ever to stay within your own ideas, to never experience anything new, or they can show you other alternatives and options. Then, once you're aware of those alternatives, you can decide if they really are for you.

A positive attitude involves several things. For starters, it means showing initiative. Too many young people sit back and wait for things to happen to them. They just don't know what it's like to make the first move and actually start something, even something that could be beneficial to themselves.

If you've acted that way in the past, its excusable. If you continue, though, you're missing one of the greatest chances not only to give to others, but also to make yourself one of those special individuals who sees possibilities, who dares to dream, and who isn't afraid of failing occasionally while moving toward a worthwhile goal. Positive attitude is often the difference between the loser and the winner, between the amateur and the professional, between the ordinary person muddling through life and the one who controls her or his existence.

To Have or Have Not   One last thought about attitude involves your ideas about those who seem to have more than you. You must realize there will always be people who are richer than you, smarter, better-looking, or who possess more authority or prestige. That's a fact of life. Don't waste a lot of your time and energy criticizing those who seem to have more than you. Accept what they have. Look at what they are, and then make your judgments. Some students from wealthy families may feel genuinely uncomfortable about their money, wishing to be more like the majority of their classmates. Some people in power would be very happy to have a day or two of relaxation, gladly giving up that power just to be able to step back and be themselves, without the responsibilities of being an authority figure.

Be smart enough to see beyond exteriors. What a person's position is or what the person has is not that important. What is inside always matters most. Learn to realize that all people have problems and sorrows, even those who seem to have it all together. Learn this, and your own attitude will mature into a more thoughtful, sensitive, and comfortable approach to life.

Self-Check

1. Give one example of what you have done lately to broaden your thinking to new attitudes and individuals.

2. On a scale of 1-10, 10 being highest, rate and explain how you think others see your openness and positive attitude.

3. Have you shown any signs of prejudice lately—racial, ethnic, sexist, ageist, religious, or otherwise?

Why or why not have these instances occurred?

4. What do you think is the most important aspect of your attitude that needs changing?

   _____

5. How could you do this? _____

6. Name one person whose attitude you admire and explain why you do.

   _____

   _____

Big Campus—
Small World

Can You Make It? Succeeding in the world of college is infinitely more demanding than making it through all the problems of high school. Because there are so many more challenges and so many more people, there is a lot more competition. There are more people who don't know you and who may not even care to know you. They're caught up in their own world, their own problems, and their own joys. That's life. Accept it.

A World of Its Own Understanding college life means understanding how completely a school can overshadow any individual's life. The campus is a world of its own. It has the ability to swallow anyone because it is such a complete atmosphere. It governs so much of not only the mind, through class and study time, but also the social, emotional, physical, and psychological lives of the people involved with it.

As they enter the "real world," many young college graduates relate how they actually lost track of what was going on while they were in school. Newspapers, radio, and TV news programs don't seem to fit in the schedule. Neither is there time for much contact with anyone outside the campus environment. Because of this, any student who is going to attempt success in college should first of all realize what a tremendous impact these years will have on him or her. It will be a total environment.

College is a place which, if you allow it, can totally consume you and hold the rest of the world at bay while you are there. Be sure your school doesn't totally absorb all your energy, your awareness, and your individuality. Remember the world of college is a stepping-stone, not a permanent patio.

How Big Is Big?

From a personal standpoint, the size of your school and its location have a great deal to do with your success in your college years.

The small campus attracts many young people because of its homelike atmosphere and the closeness individuals can feel there. A small school affords the possibility of knowing most of the students. It also provides greater opportunities for meeting instructors and professors. This promotes a feeling of being recognized as an individual rather than as just a number in some computer bank.

Yet there can be some disadvantages to the smaller school. If, for example, you need a quiet place for reflection where you can regain your perspective, the small campus can hamper those efforts because it may be harder for an individual to be anonymous. There are too many people who know you, and, as a result, you may have a harder time getting enough time to know yourself. A small campus may give an individual the feeling that he or she must live up to an image and take less time doing what he or she feels is important.

Larger schools offer greater possibility for anonymity but also have the potential for providing more opportunities of finding people who share your values and tastes. On the other hand, it's much harder for anyone to feel "at home" at a large university because there is no way one can ever really know what is going on in all the different areas of such a large school.

Get to know the people who live around you at the larger school as soon as possible. That will help. Just as neighborhoods comprise little areas of pride and comradeship in a big city, residence halls or academic departments embody small communities of self-esteem and friendship on the larger school campus. You need to feel you belong.

City Life or Small-Town Living?

If your school is located in a large city, you may not have the advantages of a sprawling, pastoral campus, and that may make other college brochures look more appealing. However, an urban school draws its life from the area surrounding it. There is much going on within walking distance or a short ride from campus. In addition, there are social and cultural events sponsored by the school. Thus, that city school derives part of its personality from where it is located. If you can learn to use and appreciate the opportunities offered by city living, you can experience a lot more than just what's in the textbooks.

On the other hand, if your school is located in or near a small town, you'll have to realize that many of the people who live in that town will have certain ideas about you, just because you're one of "those college kids." This type of college tends to influence the social life and many of the major issues confronting the local residents.

The small-town campus may influence more of your total life because you are away from home and friends. The college itself, because it is so all-inclusive, dictates what most people do in their free time, how they earn any money, and how most of them live. Your town may resent the traffic jams and the all-night parties when the football team has a home game. Just don't give them the opportunity to resent you once they've gotten to know you.

These first two examples assume that your college town is different from your hometown. However, you may be a commuting student, still living at home. There are many young people who do not "go away" to school. Today's commuter colleges, located in the suburbs or in the central cities, continue to draw more students every year. You'll read about this type of school in greater depth later on. Just remember, if you attend a college like this, you know what it is to juggle your life between home, school, community, and the part-time job you probably hold. If you commute, you may even have a tendency to feel you are not "in school" as much as your friends who go away to a large campus. You have no reason to feel this way. You have simply opted for a college situation that is giving you a taste of the real world as well as the possibilities of higher education. It will take more effort on your part to keep all aspects of your life together. However, once you learn how to do it, you also will have learned much about survival and success as a total person—a member of a family, a part-time employee, a student, and an individual.

Wherever you are in school, remember that you can control what the impact of your environment will be. Whether you are in a large or small school, the world around you is only as great or as narrow as you let it be.

Culture Shock Around the Clock

Moving into the larger college scene brings many surprises and challenges. Since you as an individual matter most, one of the first possible problems you may need to face is the acceptance of many different kinds of people, cultures, and life-styles. No matter what kind of home or high school background you may have had, entrance into the campus scene often brings a shock or two to the somewhat naive teenager as he or she meets a broader spectrum of people. As a result, you may have classmates who are old enough to be your parents, or even your grandparents! There are people from different races, cultures, countries, and certainly many individuals with values and customs that are different from your own.

Can you handle all these differences?

College is supposed to do many things for you. Obviously it is supposed to equip you with enough skill and knowledge in a certain field so that you can get and hold a good job. It is supposed to give you greater confidence in yourself by preparing to meet challenges in your future. One of the most important things college can do, however, doesn't come from studying the books. It comes from studying the people.

Because most young people's lives have been rather sheltered and limited to only a narrow world of experience, those first months of college can be eye-opening as you meet many kinds of people. Look for the good in all of them. Then, when you see something that doesn't fit or agree with your own life-style, make some decisions about how much others are going to influence you and change any of the values you hold.

When you meet the good people—the people who can help you reach and grow and make you more of a person—let them into your life. Open your mind to their thinking and at least given them a chance to tell you what is important to them and how they feel about various aspects of life.

What about the others? Eventually, you may have to leave them behind. Concentrate on the people who care about what you value and who care about you. They are the ones who will have the greatest influence on your life.

Self-Check   1. How much do you try to stay aware of what is going on in the rest of the world?

_____

Do you let the problems you face on campus get in the way of your perspective for total living?

_____

Give a detailed account of how you can stay aware of the outside world while you are in college.

_____

_____

2. What are some of the advantages you find about attending your particular school?

_____

3. How could you better take advantage of the activities and programs offered in and around your school?

_____

4. How have you tried to meet different kinds of people, and learn about different cultures and thinking?

_____

How can you do better in this regard?_____

_____

_____

Coping with Change

4

Too Young—Too Old

While college brings a lot of dilemmas, the one that seems to appear first is the simple fact that you are too old for some things and too young for others. You're certainly not a child any more, yet neither are you an adult, according to many of society's norms. Society feels you haven't paid enough dues yet. It doesn't really know how much it can expect from you, and you are still very much an unknown quantity. You're not a kid any more, yet neither are you someone who can command a lot of respect because you've gained a lot of experience. That's a Catch 22, but this one is solvable.

"I'm Becoming"

You are an adult in many ways. You have gone through a very rough mine field called high school, with not only its academic challenges, but it societal challenges as well.

You already may have made quite a few mistakes, but now you should at least be trying to get those things into perspective. You have grown up faster than any generation before you, and that gives you a certain amount of experience you can use and count on.

Going to college can throw a monkey wrench into the understanding of yourself that you took away from high school. College, which is geared toward giving you a better chance for success in the adult world, often can keep you from acting like an adult and being an adult because of its very nature. There are a lot of rules you are expected to obey because there are a lot of people around. Often these rules presume many college students can't handle all situations with the greatest amount of good judgment. Since you are a student, these rules affect you, and they can be the first proving ground as to the measure of maturity you have already gained.

Demands in the academic arena similarly presume you don't always have the drive or ability to learn on your own. The organization of your particular grading system still insists on measuring in some way how well you achieve—or fail. There are no report cards or grades in the adult world, though. There is simply the knowledge within each person that success has come.

Time for You

Because of its many obligations, demands, and rules, college may force you to think too much about yourself. Normal living is a give-and-take situation and involves a certain amount of awareness of others. Adulthood carries with it responsibility and obligations to others. Because right now the focus is on you—on your potential, your ability to measure up to standards, and your willingness to work up the motivation to achieve specific goals and skills—you may be caught up in what some people consider the luxury of thinking only of yourself.

As you move through these college years, you will have to spend a lot of time on yourself. You'll have to do many things that will prove your ability to succeed, both as a student and as a person. You can do yourself a big favor, though, by not letting collegiate demands force you to forget about others. Young children believe the world revolves around them. That lets them get away with a lot of unacceptable behavior because it seems cute in childhood.

The adult, on the other hand, realizes that no one is in the center of anything except his or her own life. Life consists of many individuals constantly revolving around each other, sometimes giving and sometimes taking. Learning the balance of that delicate dance of life is one of the first things you should try to accomplish during these college years.

Growth: An Ongoing Process

Look back at a lot of the growing you accomplished during high school, and even earlier. Recognize the good learning and the successes you achieved over books and over your own problems. While society seems aware of your inexperience, you should realize that you do have a lot of good experience behind you already. You've grown; you've changed. You've discarded certain parts of your life that are no longer important, and you've replaced them with values and goals, and even dreams, that are a vital part of you now. Look back at the things of youth you've laid aside, the advances in maturity you've made, and the growth of your ability to separate the important from the fringe areas of your life.

Take a look at yourself and see how strong you've become in at least a few areas of your life. Look at your growing independence and ability to deal with people. Appreciate your openness to new experiences and different ideas, which you've proven by enrolling in college. Reading books like this also show you are on the right track of motivation and desire. These are good things, and you may not be acknowledging them enough. Then look around at what you can change in your life now.

Is the dorm one of your least favorite places to be? Maybe you should look into a sorority or fraternity, or, as soon as you're able, the possibility of living off campus.

Are the people you've settled in with really your kind of people? Or do they have a tendency to draw you away from things you like?

How about your major or your feelings about developing one? Now that your personality has developed even more and your abilities are beginning to show themselves in more mature fashion, is that career you've chosen or want to explore really right for you?

Making some changes now may be painful and may even seem to set you back, but making them now is easier than ripping up an even more established life later on. Adulthood is reached when you have the ability to make almost constant changes, always refining and redefining yourself and your abilities.

There are, of course, some things you can't change once you've set them in motion. You may have already set some of your major goals for school, and that should give you some direction. If you know, for example, that an important exam is coming before you are accepted into a specialized training program, you know you'll have to keep on top of the studies required. You can also save yourself the tension you would otherwise feel if you approached such an exam poorly prepared.

You've already been asked to do many things you don't like doing. It started at home. It moved through all your schooling and in any jobs you've had so far. It has even happened with your friends and those with whom you socialize. But at this point you know it's simply a part of life one has to accept and deal with as best as possible. College now sets a whole new set of requirements before you, and you need to accept these changes.

You can, on the one hand, take the sophomoric attitude that you won't meet these new requirements, that you are above them. Some do that. Those people also never reach their goals, let alone college graduation day.

Instead, you can make the decision to go ahead and complete the necessary tasks and give them the most energy you can muster. You have your goals. You have your ambitions. Meeting your goals means paying some dues, and these requirements are some of those dues. Realize that, and also realize that by filling those requirements you are selling out neither yourself nor any of your values. You are simply acting like a member of a very large club called the human race!

Great Expectations

People do expect a lot from you, don't they? The people who are on the fringe of your life as classmates or friends expect you to have your mind made up on your general approach to life. Professors, graduate assistants, and parents seem to keep expecting your best, sometimes not realizing you aren't always up to giving your best. Most people presume you have a purpose and a goal. They expect you to study, they expect you to learn, and they presume you will succeed.

Younger teenagers also expect you to have it all together. They admire you and envy you because you made it through high school. They see your life as so much freer than theirs. In fact, all they see is your freedom and your mobility. They don't see the new pressures you have or the sometimes staggering demands that are made on you.

Show 'Em!   What can you do? One part of the world sees you as inexperienced and untested. It questions almost every move you make. Another part of that same world envies you and expects nothing short of greatness. And there you are in the middle. Some good changes have already occurred, and many more are still ahead.

To make your life easier and more successful, just be yourself. Share some of your doubts and frustrations with the people who are important to you. Let them see that you don't have all the answers but that you are determined to find them. Let them see a calmness in you, recognizing growth and the changes that have already happened. Make them aware that your future is a very special and sacred place for you. Let them know that you realize you've made a few mistakes here and there but that you've learned from them, too. Give others a peek at the "you" that exists in all honesty.

Also be honest with yourself. Accept your basic goodness and your ability to succeed at least most of the time. The more positive and honest you can be about yourself, the more positively everyone else will react to you. And the most positive reactions you get, the greater and more successful you will become.

Self-Check   1. Which of your school's rules do you detest most? _____

_____

How can you abide by them with the least amount of stress to you?

_____

_____

2. On a scale of 1–10, 10 being the highest, how would you rate the quality of time you spend with friends and classmates?

_____

How could you make it better? _____

_____

3. Have you met people who are at your level of maturity, motivation, and willingness to approach college seriously?

   _____

   What are you doing to keep these friends, or what can you do to find them?

   _____

   _____

4. Name an instance that proves you've grown in maturity, personality, and mental outlook. Explain your example.

   _____

   _____

   _____

   _____

5. Do others realize you've reached certain levels of maturity and motivation toward specific goals? What can you do to let them know?

   _____

   _____

Calling Your Own Shots

Don't Play Games—Take Aim!

A big math exam is only two days away, and you're still behind on a few assignments. It's definitely midnight oil time, but someone down the hall has a great party planned. Everyone will be there. But that exam is going to affect your final grade in a major way. What to do?

One of the biggest challenges of college, especially if this is the first time you are more or less on your own, is that you have only yourself to make the right decisions. Many people will try to influence you now and all through your life, but when the door is shut and you are alone, the decision to study or not, as well as the decision to do anything, rests solely and completely on your shoulders.

Can you handle the freedom every adult has to handle? Can you make the right decisions?

The War for Independence

If you have looked upon your life, especially those rugged high school years, as a continuing war for independence, you may be in a bit of trouble. During those years you won a few battles and so did your folks, your teachers, and any other authority figures in your life.

That whole situation, however, wasn't really a war. There were simply people who were concerned that you couldn't handle everything, and who, as a result, didn't trust you to make your own right decisions. They meant well. Try to believe that.

Now the pendulum has swung to the other extreme. Whether you are on campus or still living at home, your parents probably expect you to make more of your own decisions. If you are on campus, you simply have to. No one is holding your hand or looking over your shoulder.

Somehow you must have noticed your folks' attitude toward you changing. You have more freedom now. In fact, most of the adults in your life seem more interested in what you're doing and what you're thinking. They can tell by your actions that you are changing and meeting new and different situations.

Most people realize you are approaching adulthood, and as they face that fact, they may even unconsciously change their attitude toward you. They may begin to expect more of you, too. They will begin to ask your opinions more often, and they'll expect you to have some good reasoning and mature judgment behind those opinions.

One of the most basic human needs is freedom. In fact, there are many people who feel they can never be free enough! There's a difference, though, between freedom and another word—license. License means total freedom—freedom even from responsibility. It's a freedom to be yourself without thinking about others or the consequences of your actions. License means doing exactly as you please, whenever and whatever. It may give you a feeling of liberty, but license always implies a certain amount of irresponsibility, selfishness, and lack of concern for others or for what is realistic or right.

True freedom, on the other hand, is an independent kind of maturity. It gives you the ability to make your own decisions, to be your own person. At the same time, however, it involves maturity and retaining an awareness of others. Independence is not winning a war against anyone, any law, or any authority figure. If there is any battle involved in freedom, it's a battle against one's own immaturity and selfishness. That's where the real conflict can occur, and where the real victory is won.

Where do you begin?

Don't Be a Tourist

There are many different kinds of people. Every one of them has a different personality. They come from different environments, and they all have different aptitudes and different motivation. How well you blend in with others while maintaining your own individuality is up to you.

Too many people are only followers. They are tourists in their own lives, stopping along the way to see surface things and nothing more. They make sure they have their adequate share of pleasure and entertainment, and they do all they can to amass as much money as possible and buy as many material goods as possible. They go through the motions of being adults, but they have never really won that war for independence inside themselves. Freedom from valuing things above people and one's own worth is one of the greatest freedoms of all.

People who are leaders in society remain in the minority. They very often become leaders in their own lives as well as in others' lives. They stand out as individuals—persons who are on top of their own thinking and whose perspective is clear and forward-looking. They are unique and special because they are not afraid to be themselves.

As you go through the stages before graduation and your career, this may be your last opportunity to set some good and workable patterns for the rest of your life. True, when you were a young teen, freedom meant staying out as long as you wished or having the liberty to do what you wanted with your own time. Now, however, your time is all your own, though with your current demands you may not feel that way.

There's your job, and if you live at home and commute to a local school, there is still the time you choose to spend with your family. If you live in a dorm or on campus, there must be time for your social life, too. No matter where you live, there must always be time for study and class preparation. The freedom is there to use your time as you wish. The problem is, how do you apportion it among the many activities you value?

Independence is a state of mind. Freedom is not something you win; it's something that grows inside of you until it becomes part of your personality. Independence is just knowing how to take care of yourself, and at the same time staying aware of others and your obligations to them. True independence comes from accepting yourself, trying to change the things you don't like about yourself and having enough confidence in yourself so that you are not swayed by every new idea and new person you encounter.

Your personality has evolved, and it is still evolving. One of the first places you can begin to assert your inde-

pendence is by being true to that personality. If you don't
need to be around people all the time, don't let others
make you feel you should be. Let your own personality, as
it evolves, be evident to the people around you. Let them
see the real you—what you care about, what you feel, and
what is important to you. The more people become aware
of your own preferences and opinions, the less they'll try to
put their own words in your mouth.

How easily do you buckle under when others pressure
you? How important, in fact, is acceptance from others?
True, people need people, and you are probably not called
to be a hermit. You are, on the other hand, called to be
yourself! There may be some lonely times while you continue to search for your kind of people. Maybe you need to
change your routine a little or get involved in a few different activities to find them. But keep looking, because your
kind of people are out there.

Take Command You can opt at this point to be a follower, or you can grab
hold of that person in the mirror and begin to let the world
see how terrific he or she really is.

Although you probably have some rough edges yet, have
courage to be your true self. Look at the successes you've
had already, not so much with things, but with people. Look
at the friends who have really cared about you and the people who have opened up to you. Look at how far you've
come, and you'll get more courage to go on even farther.

The college system, your friends, your family, your employer, and anyone connected with your life can make demands on you. You will have to do many things you really
don't like, and you'll have to spend some time giving up
your own preferences once in a while to achieve some
greater goal. That's normal.

On the other hand, no one can demand from you the one
thing that is most essential—for you to be your true self,
independent enough to keep others from stereotyping you
or telling you how to live your life.

If you think you have an image on campus, part of asserting your independence will be to break that image into
a thousand pieces, forcing others to see you not as a stereotype, but as a unique individual. High school may have
been a place where individuals needed the security of
groups and cliques, but you are beyond that now.

One good thing about college is that it's a whole new
world, and it changes often enough for you to change with

it. If you have been in school for a year or two, you can still change your image with a new group of people you meet in a particular class, or with newcomers to your dorm, fraternity, or sorority. Independence is not something one achieves and then holds. It is rather a constant refining of the real you—and the you that is coming into being. It's starting to be yourself and then starting over and over again as you continue to change.

Be comfortable with yourself. Like yourself. You'll find most people liking you and learning to be comfortable with the person they see. Don't push your opinions and preferences on others. However, at the same time, let others know you're not an easy target for their attempts to influence you.

Simple, isn't it? Try it. You may like yourself a lot more, and that will be half the battle.

Self-Check

1. How able do you think others feel you are to make your own decisions and lead your own life?

   _____

   Give an example.

   _____

   _____

2. What are the three greatest areas of freedom in your life right now?

   _____

   _____

   _____

   Describe how well you are using them. _____

3. Do you consider yourself a follower or a leader? _____

   Why? _____

   _____

4. Identify one of your greatest personal successes, and give reasons why it happened.

_____

_____

_____

5. What are your two most likable qualities, and how successful are you at letting others be aware of them?

_____

_____

_____

_____

How to Be Good to Yourself

6

Filling in the Blanks

Lots of people throughout your life may have tried to tell you what you need and what you should want from life. They may have meant well, but to find out what you really need, you should know by now there is only one place to turn—to yourself!

You need friends and happiness. You need success and the feeling you are getting somewhere. You need to feel good about yourself, just as you need to feel good about certain aspects of your life. You deserve happiness. What you need more than anything, however, is an honest and realistic acceptance of yourself.

One of the hardest things to do in college is to maintain control of everything. That includes yourself, your room and possible roommate, your relationships, your classes, and your battle with the books. This presumes a bit of confidence on your part, and some recognition of your past successes. It presumes you've learned some independence, too.

There may be a certain amount of rebelliousness in you right now; the college system certainly offers plenty to feel rebellious about. But don't drain all your mental and psychological resources trying to totally revamp the college system. It has been there before you, and it will be there after you're gone. Fighting it may do nothing but make you bitter or cynical. Just change your college's impact and importance in your own life and try to work with what's there. The real battle is won in your perspective and in what you take away from these short years of school.

Your youth is an advantage. One quality, which many older adults envy, is your ability to be idealistic. False idealism can put your head in the clouds and take you away from reality, but an honest attempt at making things the best they can be will give you an ability to struggle for what you think is right.

Friend or Foe?

When pressure from study or just the normal demands of time or work get you down, there is nothing like a good friend who can make life happy again or bring it back to a brighter perspective.

Many people speak of winning friends, and that seems to set up some false impressions for some. No one wins friends the same way he or she wins a trophy or a contest. Friends are a gift, and they often come from unexpected sources. Friendship has very little to do with mental or social equality. It is a mystery, a certain chemistry that works between two people who might even seem to be very different, but who share some common bond. Your good friends will be people who share your own degree of sensitivity, and they will be strong enough in themselves to forget their own individuality once in a while and offer you honest, sincere caring.

Friendship is never easy. There are times when it brings a lot of joy and makes you aware of great beauty. There are also times it demands almost more than you feel you can or want to give. Truly mature people may not have many friends, but those they have are like solid gold. These friends are the people who really know them and care for them, perhaps even in spite of themselves!

You may feel those good friends are still missing from your life. You may have left some back at high school graduation. Maybe you have many acquaintances who share the surface things with you, but you still may be looking for those special individuals who can see beneath the surface and appreciate your qualities and your special needs.

Keep searching! The search is never easy, and the wait may be a lonely one, but it's always worth it. If you look around a bit, especially on the college campus where there are so many people with so many different backgrounds, you will certainly find some kindred souls. They may be involved in the same activities you like; that will give you a launching point from which friendships may begin to develop.

Success: How Right Is the Price?

Another one of your most basic needs all through life will be the need for success. A person who constantly sees himself or herself as a failure, not only with things, but also with people, will be truly miserable.

You may not feel as successful as you desire when grades come out. Maybe you feel pressure to constantly remain on the dean's list or prove something to the folks back home. If you let it, this can become an almost overwhelming problem.

Some people measure success by the amount of money or prestige they acquire. That's unfortunate for two reasons. First, it doesn't account for the greatest success of all—success within the human spirit. Second, it tends to drive people into too many critical judgments of themselves. What others think of you and how they assess you will always remain a factor in your life, and you are only normal to want to prove to them that you possess certain talents and abilities.

The most important success, however, is the success you feel within yourself. Very often it may not be seen by others or totally understood by them. You should realize it's there, though, and acknowledge it often. This success as a person can be determined by how well you see yourself acting and reacting to people and situations around you. You won't always be the terrific person others expect. You'll have your bad days. Yet if you can see an honesty in your manner of living, an attempt at being your true self and remaining a productive person, you will find a lot of success within and around yourself.

The opinions of people you care about will obviously be important. Listen to them, and weigh their judgments with a certain amount of seriousness, but never think they are infallible. *You* know yourself best.

Go back through those years again and notch a few successes in your belt. Then look at the success you've had in recent weeks and months. Just the fact you are still making it, still surviving, still "hanging in there" in spite of all the pressures and demands on you is a success in itself.

To assure the possibility of success up ahead, there are a few tips you can remember.

- Set a few realistic goals. Give yourself something to shoot for instead of just drifting from semester to semester. Take an honest look at your abilities and potential, and set goals that are within reach. And not all those goals should be aimed at some vague time in the future. A lot of smaller goals, which can be achieved in the weeks or months ahead, will give you that feeling of continuing success you need right now. If you know you can succeed in the small things, it won't take much effort to develop some confidence when aiming at your larger goals.

- Give yourself the opportunity to see your accomplishments, to know you're getting somewhere. Take a look at what you've learned in a particular course, or how your friendship with a certain individual has developed and matured. Remember your relationship with your family from a few years ago and applaud any changes that have occurred for the better.

- Judge yourself, but don't automatically accept others' judgments of you. Many people tend to be negative and critical. You are much too important to treat yourself that way. Don't put yourself down or criticize yourself without giving yourself an honest chance for success.

- Accept what is, change what you can, then live according to standards that you know are right and workable for you.

Will success come? No one can answer that, not even you. All you can do is give it your best shot. Try your hardest, and do what you feel is necessary to achieve each goal you set for yourself. Doing that, in itself, may be the greatest personal success of all!

Inventory

1. How do you rate your loyalty to friends? _____

   Give an example of a recent time you acted like a reliable, caring friend.

   _____

2. Name a goal you can achieve in the next six months, then detail what it will take to reach it.

   _____

   _____

   _____

3. What changes do you need to make in your life right now to assure some of your goals will be fullfilled?

   _____

   _____

Naive? Roll Up Your Sleeves!

You may have led an insulated life during high school, but that's about to change. You know you must face the reality of your world as it is, and you must develop your own personal way of dealing with it.

If you feel you were too naive when you walked into your first college class, learn to get over the culture shock. The diversity of people and the complexity of demands in college can be almost overwhelming to many students facing new situations, new temptations and new dilemmas. Yet all these can be faced with calm reality.

There is no one keeping the truth away in college. Instead, there is only the task of sifting through it all and learning how to deal with it as it comes. That's all you can do, and that is all that life demands.

A New Set of Problems

Filling in the blanks in your life at this point should involve understanding the problems you bring to college with you, as well as facing the new ones you find. The time for naivete is over.

If there is trouble at home, for example, that trouble has not gone away because you aren't there to see it. It is taking its toll on those still at home, and whether you know it or not, it is also still taking a psychological toll on you. Pain has a way of not going away. If there are problems back at home or with old friends, you'll have to continue to deal with them at a distance. You never stop being part of your family. Keep room in your life for them, even if it involves a long-distance phone bill.

Next, you have brought *yourself* to school, and you may be one of your biggest problems. If you are aware of some glaring personality problem that was evident from time to time in high school, that trait is probably still there. You must deal with it eventually. You'll never have the time to address it as you do now. Stop letting it have such impact in your life.

Your attitudes toward a variety of issues may be changing, but you should know they are still very much a part of you. Do you see any problems in your basic values? Only you can recognize them in your moments of honesty and make some plans for trying to tackle them.

Also, there is the problem of you and others. Some young people sense and many adults believe that lack of communication skills is the biggest obstacle to success among college students. Because their narrow world consisted of friends, family, and a few outsiders who wandered through periodically, many high school graduates suffer from a severe lack of experience in dealing with diverse people.

Many employers shake their heads and complain that too many college graduates don't know how to talk or meet people. They testify that many young employees remain silent much too often when their opinions are asked and they never feel confident enough to contribute to a conversation, let alone a situation that demands new ideas or creative thinking.

What is the source of this problem? It's that narrow world that has kept so many young people from dealing honestly with others. There may have never been a need to speak that much. Since no one has ever expected you to be assertive and communicative before, you may be at a loss once strangers and outsiders start looking for more than you're used to giving. This may be leading to a lack of confidence on your part. Therefore, as your college years progress, it might be wise to force yourself into situations where you will need to talk more and deal with new people in a more confident and assertive way.

Speak Up!

Many young people feel it isn't their place to speak first or to give any indication of a willingness to talk by either a smile or even a nod. If you still think that way, it's time to change your way of thinking! Others very often don't know how to deal with you and, rather than make that extra effort to relate to you, they may tend to ignore you or simply tell you what *they* want. Then, seeing your lack of confidence, they will just presume you agree with them.

If college is doing anything at all, it should be making you a more assertive individual. You have a lot to contribute to any situation. There are good thoughts in your head, and the world needs to hear them. Let people know you aren't just another follower. Let them see you as a confident, creative, and assertive person.

When necessary, confront people in a gentle but strong way. Speak your mind and never fear the possible rejection. If people reject you, they have simply not seen the goodness and worthiness in you. That's their problem. Don't let it be yours!

Talk. Smile. Let others know you're there and that you're ready to communicate. You'll find a lot of your problems melting away once you can establish yourself as an alive, vibrant, and assertive individual. Don't wait for the world to knock on your door. Open the door yourself, and let it see the growing goodness inside!

Realize Where You've Been

Society—that big world out there—feels it knows many things about you, and one of the things it feels most sure of is your lack of experience. At first thought, you may tend to agree with this, knowing you haven't had a lot of opportunities to confront situations or to prove yourself. Society tends to feel experience comes only with age and with facing different situations on a day-to-day basis. In that respect, it is right about you. You do lack that kind of experience.

Yet what about all the other kinds of experiences you have had? You have dealt with people. You had the experience of meeting the challenge of high school and the part of college that is already behind you. You have grown up quickly in a demanding world. If you've begun to break down that communication gap between you and the rest of the world, you've also had the experience of meeting some different people and of sharing your ideas with others who come from diverse backgrounds.

What you are lacking in the field of work experience you have already begun to fill up with something much more important—experience in active living.

Because your preteen and teen years have been hectic, you have had the opportunity of making decisions and of confronting various sides of life, values, and attitudes at an early age. You have probably gone through some really difficult situations already and experienced many of the deepest human emotions. You've had to retain your love and positive attitude when others have forced pain or rejection on you, and you have overcome those hard times. Many adults don't appreciate that, and you may have to teach them a few facts about your life in as gentle and positive a way as possible. Showing them by your actions will be the best lesson of all.

If you can honestly look at the blank spots in your life, acknowledge them, and begin to fill them up, you can take the first step toward acceptance as a worthwhile individual. Many adults are sitting back, waiting for the first sign that you are mature and confident enough to take your place beside them in the world. They know you have a lot to offer. They probably even envy your talents and your training. They're just afraid you don't know how to offer what you have. Show them!

Don't be afraid to speak and share your opinions, always remembering the circumstances and sensitivities of others. Don't let yourself be a follower all the time. Be an initiator once in a while, a person who sees the job, offers an analysis, and then suggests ways of getting it done. Let people know you understand the problems in your life, the pressures you feel, the demands for your time, the pull from possible problems at home. Let them know you also see the possibilities that lie ahead, and make them sure you feel you can deal with it all.

There are many blanks in your life right now, but you can fill them up by beginning to take command. You can let the world know that now only you exist, but that you have something worthwhile to offer. Believe in yourself. It won't take long before the rest of the world learns to believe in you, too.

Self-Check   1. On a scale of 1–10, 10 being the highest, how would you rate your ability to communicate with others?

   _____

   What are the biggest reasons you can't communicate on the level you would like?

   _____

What can you do about it in the next month? _____

_____

2. Do you focus more on the past or the future? _____

How can you keep yourself excited about the future and its possibilities? Be specific.

_____

_____

3. What is one of the happiest successes you can remember?

_____

_____

4. How can you overcome any sense of past failure? _____

_____

5. How would you describe your perspective on life now?

_____

_____

THE NITTY GRITTY

Part II

Learning to Function

Do Not Pass Goal   Crunch time. Everyone else around you is busy doing
something. The campus looks serene enough. But now
comes that gnawing feeling from somewhere deep inside.

    It's time to produce. How can you begin or carry on with
the rest of your college life successfully? Understand as
much as you can about your situation.

The Minisociety   First of all, realize that college is a minisociety, and you
are a member of it. The more you understand about your-
self and why you are here, the better you'll be able to cope
with any demand, ride with pressure, and get all that this
particular college or university can give you. College is, after all, just a scaled-down version of the way it is in the
world. There are people who make laws, and at least some

who enforce those laws. There are the leaders, the artists and poets, the dreamers and thinkers, the finely tuned minds that chart technical or qualitative progress. There are those who work best with people and whose talent lies in encouraging others to be more productive.

There are losers, too. They're in society; and your college, no matter how hard it tries to weed them out, has its share, too. These are the people who are going through the motions but who are neither productive nor positive. They probably are not making much of a contribution to your school or to their own development. Learn to stay clear of them. They have a tendency to not like being alone, and they'll drag down anyone who will join them on their slide toward mediocrity or failure.

If you can learn to function with a certain amount of autonomy and direction in the midst of all these people on your campus, you'll probably succeed very well. You'll also walk away after graduation with a real handle on the future.

Bromide for the College Blues

If you are going to get the most out of these years, you can do a few things to ensure that your success will be not just getting by, but a victory of honest growth. Develop some realistic goals. Have specific purposes for the classes you take, even if the purpose is nothing more than learning to enjoy things more.

Although doing just enough to get by may have seemed acceptable in high school, college can't be approached that way. You may have done very well by getting by in your local high school, but college includes a type of competition you may never have known before. It is a stepping-stone, and because of that, you must stay aware of the future and consider what those years up ahead may require. For the students who have no particular goals and who are in school solely because their parents want them there or because that's where all their old friends went, classes and the whole campus scene can quickly become a drag and not worth the trouble.

If you feel yourself losing interest in school, here's one quick remedy: plan some options and goals. With a purpose in mind, you'll be able to tolerate a lot more, and you'll learn more, too. Ease yourself into really knowing where you're headed. You don't have to plot out your entire life in these few years. All you need to do is plan a few options for yourself. And the first plan is to attend class and stay in school!

The Times Certainly Are Changing!

You may think you're preparing for your life's work, the career that will cover all your professional life, and you may be right. Remember, however, life is a changing thing, and as long as you have breath in you, you'll change, too. Teach yourself to live with change now. Because the years ahead will be quite different, there's a chance you will be different, too. What you learn now—your skills and your knowledge—will always serve you well. Just be realistic enough to know that you are laying a foundation and that the final edifice may turn out to be something you can't even imagine right now.

Watch the Curves

There are many people who, in their late thirties or forties, give up their original careers and turn their lives completely around. They go into totally different work areas or life-styles because they feel that's what is best for them at that point in their lives. You may someday join them. Consider that, and at least prepare yourself for the possibilities the world may offer you. Just be sure there will always be new challenge and the need for newer knowledge up ahead as the world continues to grow and refine itself.

One of the growing problems of the work world is an increasing boredom on the part of workers and management. Many people tend to lose interest in their jobs after a few years because they see no challenge in them any more. They feel they've done as much as they can do and begin to look elsewhere for new motivation and professional stimulation. They remember youthful dreams and wonder if they've made the right choices with their lives. Sometimes they actually decide it's time for change and move on.

This may happen to you in the future. Accept that possibility, and let yourself feel the inner strength you have to deal with the changes, whether they are forced on you or you choose them. Remember that no one expects you to plan your whole life in one or four years. All anyone can realistically hope is that you learn as much as you can, set some goals for the immediate future, grow as much as possible, and become as positive, flexible, and adaptable as you can be. The individual who can easily ride the winds of change will be the real winner in his or her adult years. That person will also be one of the happiest and most realistic individuals around!

Read Reality   Freshmen usually come to campus genuinely nervous, but optimistic. They have a high level of confidence, knowing they've succeeded in high school. They expect to do the same in college, once they learn their way around. That's good. A high level of confidence is one of the better assets to carry into any new venture. Some freshmen, however, because they want to be aware of everything, expect too much too soon and tend to scatter their energies. One of the best things a freshman can learn as quickly as possible is that there are still only twenty-four hours in every day.

Older students should be more realistic and selective about their goals. One would hope that, by the later years of college, an individual has stopped playing games and has become not less fun-loving, but more serious about the future and the possibilities it holds. By junior or senior year, a student can begin to assess the quality of his or her education. That is a good time to judge growth in professional as well as personal skill areas.

How seriously do you approach your classes? Do you just want to pass or are you really there to learn? You can, you know, try to make it through college with as many light-content classes as possible. You can use that same mentality to get through life. On the other hand, you can take the most college can offer and expect the most from life by helping yourself get a real education. Specific skills are needed now more than ever.

Take Charge   You are an individual. Accept that fact and be proud of it!

True, you'll have to bend a little to fit into the college system, just as you always will have to bend to a certain extent in life. Just remember, college is there for you, not you for it. If pressures and demands seem to be making you tense, it may be time to sit down and reassess your goals and how much you can give to achieving them.

You do have a few options. No one expects you to go through college feeling overworked, tense, and unable to live a fairly normal life. There must be time for yourself, just as there should be time to do what you feel is necessary to your total development as a person. There should be time to date, if you wish, time to be with your friends, and a weekend once in a while when you feel free to leave the books and campus behind and visit the folks or old friends.

One suggestion is to look at your schedule. You may have signed up for too many classes. You may have misjudged your ability to handle so many hours per semester or quarter. If you are into your schedule already, you may decide to stay with it until the end of the grading period. You should also consider dropping any class that you feel is taking too much out of you. Your sanity does count for something!

Even if it means a later graduation date, it may be better to lighten your work load. If you are too tense, consider taking fewer hours each semester. Your own schedule will show you how many lab classes and how many heavy classes you need to take. If you can space the demanding classes over several semesters, you may find handling the responsibilities of those classes a lot easier.

Stopping Out

If the total college system seems to be getting to you in a more serious way, you may even consider what some think is a drastic action. "Stopping out"—taking a semester or a year off from school—may help you in the long run. If you are at the point of total frustration and see no value in college or have no goal toward which you can work with a strong sense of direction, taking some time off from school to get out into the work world may be just what you need to establish a clearer perspective. By working, you'll get an idea of what life after college will be like. It may help you decide whether you want to go on with school, and how much you can expect from it. It can also help you assess how much effort you are willing to spend for that college diploma.

If you feel such an action may be imminent in your life, stopping out will give you a better idea of alternatives that lie ahead. For example, you may decide you'll be just as content working in a job that doesn't demand a college degree. You may also decide there is no way in the world you want to do that type of work for the rest of your life!

Either way, stopping out may be a healthy alternative to continuing on in a frustrating situation. A semester or a year off can help you get your head together and should make college a lot easier to endure, once you know what you want and how willing you are to pay the price it demands. If others don't understand your decision on this, help them understand. It's time to live your own life, and it's about time you started living it with a fair amount of intelligent independence.

You Need Your Own Kindness

Above all, look at what is expected of you. Change what you can change until you feel you are able to do your best with each class. Then make decisions with your own best interests, both present and future, in mind. College can be an enjoyable as well as an educational experience, but you must help make it so. Don't be afraid to tailor-make your schedule to fit your needs. Let others know you will try your best but that, as you go through a certain program or curriculum, you must also keep yourself sane and enjoy the growing.

Adulthood, once it comes, should be enjoyable. But if you have spent your college years tense, frustrated, and constantly under pressure, you may not be able to enjoy your adult years either.

Be as demanding of yourself as you realistically can be, but in the last analysis, be good to yourself. Real success always carries more happiness than tension with it.

Self-Check

1. Name three specific goals you can reach by the end of this year.

   _____

   _____

   _____

2. What is your most difficult class? _____

3. Suggest two things you can do to meet the work load this class demands. How could you make it better?

   _____

   _____

4. On a scale of 1–10, 10 being the most realistic, rate how realistic your class load is now.

   _____

5. If you would like to cut down or add classes, what is preventing you?

   _____

6. Assess your ability to cope with the pressures of college.

   _____

7. Have you considered dropping out or stopping out? _____ What would be your reasons for taking or not taking these actions, and how realistic are they in your total plan for the future?

   _____

   _____

   _____

8. Give three items of advice to anyone who feels too much tension from the college scene.

   _____

   _____

   _____

Attacking the Class Load

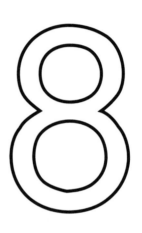

8

Methods for Class Management

If it's true that an army runs on its stomach, it is also true that any college is either as good or as mediocre as its classes and what those classes provide for students. You have already read about students who really want to learn and those who are simply out for the diploma. But is it possible for a school to offer both, and for any normal student to achieve both?

Yes, if you are willing to help educate yourself. And before you say, "I'll be glad for the diploma, thank you!"— read on.

The college diploma these days carries a meaning of accomplishment, as it always has. Yet when the job market is tight and many companies are cutting down on personnel in middle management and every other sector, that diploma will get you in the door.

What you learned to get that diploma will become critical, and while employers won't expect you to know everything it will take to work for them, they want to know you've gained the basic groundwork. They will do the acclimation to any job they give you, but they'll expect you to have some idea of what you're doing. While the diploma may say you gained the credits and won the approval of a college or university, it is the approval of those who are running the business where you want to work that you need the most.

Many high school students are notorious for sitting back and letting others choose their classes, choose their teachers, and, in the long run, choose the direction of their education. College puts much more responsibility on you, expecting you to know yourself well enough to have decided on a major by the end of sophomore year, as well as some future goals.

Risk Being a Pest

Being on your own often can be frustrating when you first hit the college scene. For example, counselors and advisors won't call you in, as your high school teachers did. They presume you know they are there, willing to help when you need them. Not using your advisor is a mistake; he or she is in a real position to help. Unless you go and perhaps even persistently ask for help, your advisor may feel you are on the right track and let you go along through semester after semester. This is especially true in large universities where, because of the large number of students, it is impossible for any counselor to take a personal interest in every person on his or her list.

It's up to you to take that interest in the most important person—yourself!

Let your advisor or counselor get to know you as an individual. Let that person see where you are at present and where you hope to go. It will be up to you to request an appointment, but that will be energy well spent. Run the risk of becoming a permanent fixture in the counseling offices, but get the help you need.

Too many college students feel they have to do almost all of their own planning. They may consult the folks back home, but Mom and Dad may not have a real idea of what's going on at school. They probably don't know the requirements or curriculum well enough to help you make the best judgments.

Counselors do. They know optional classes and various programs, and they can often suggest electives that will help you meet your long-range goals. Most college counselors usually know their business, but unfortunately some are underworked because students choose not to use their services. Don't make that mistake. Let your advisor help you understand more of what the school expects of you and what you can expect from your school in the way of real education.

Lightweight, Middleweight, Heavyweight

Organizing your schedule for a semester or quarter of work is a serious project. As you move through college, each time you select classes, you should do it with greater knowledge of yourself and a better understanding of the curriculum. Don't just haphazardly fill up your schedule. It's going to consume the better part of your time for several months. Make it work for you.

You may have a tendency to take general courses that will still count toward your major. You can get decent grades in these, but you may learn little in the specific skill ability potential employers will expect from you. What you want is knowledge! Try to find professors who have some practical experience in the subjects they are teaching. They'll not only give you the basic information you need, they'll also be able to give you many inside tips on specifics because they know firsthand what you'll find once you actually land a job.

Your work load can be made a lot easier if you mix heavy and light classes. Talk to others who have taken a class or who know the requirements of a particular professor. How many papers does he or she assign? What are the outside assignments like? How much reading is involved? Find out, if possible, who the instructor in each of your classes will be. Demanding instructors, who require much outside reading and many papers, will ask a lot of your time and a lot of your effort. You'll have to decide if you're up to meeting their requirements.

A little tip: if you know a certain professor will be conducting a class you must take, and you've heard about his or her reputation for being demanding and a difficult grader, make sure you take the class during a semester when you also have a few electives that will not require too much work. Dancing, art, scuba diving, individual sports, or public speaking may all be classes that don't involve a lot of outside work, and which can actually add to your enjoyment while you're at school.

Above all, keep your options open. Don't lock yourself into an irrevocable regimen of classes. Unless you are absolutely sure of your major, leave a few alternatives as you plan classes and electives. It may save you a few headaches and worry about credits later on as you get closer to graduation.

Some Class Notes   There is no way anyone can study for you or make you understand a class. However, there are ways you can help yourself, especially in larger classes where you may feel like a blade of grass out in left field.

You'll receive a class plan from most professors or teaching assistants. Sometimes it may be worth an hour or two to read ahead to understand the particular theme or orientation of that class.

At the beginning of each course it helps to find out when test dates are scheduled and what kind of tests these will be. Will they be multiple choice or fact tests where you know you'll have to understand terms and their definitions, as well as a lot of details? Will they be theme or essay tests? That will take more total understanding of a subject, and by knowing such tests are coming, you can be more aware of the class as a whole, and keep a total picture of how the material is being developed.

Most professors have a theme to their lectures. Recognize that theme as soon as possible and ask some general questions about it. This will not only make the professor aware of you, it will also help you understand what he or she considers important.

Once you have found the main idea of a class, base your notes on that theme. Writing down fragments of information will do little good unless the instructor also is fragmented! If the prof seems to wander through a subject day after day, she or he probably will ask you to remember the facts that have been mentioned time after time. A good lecturer, however, will have a theme, and once you understand her or his objectives for the class, it will be much easier to follow and understand the direction of the lectures.

Sitting near the front in a lecture room helps, too. Instructors will learn your face and name much more quickly. Combine this with a few good questions from time to time, and the instructor soon will become aware of you as a person. You can be sure many individuals will sit back and say nothing for the majority of class time. Even when discussion is encouraged, they'll stay silent. These people may feel they learn best by listening, but if you can overcome a tendency toward shyness and ask enough questions to let an instructor know you're interested and are trying to learn, you'll not only help your grade, you will also help yourself get that real education you've been reading about in this book.

If you find yourself in a large class in which you are placed in an auxiliary room, listening only to a set of speakers, hang on. You will soon enough get into classes that are more manageable in size. In the meantime, find a teaching assistant and ask the questions you have. Meeting for a study group with others in your class will also get you beyond the feeling of being a number instead of a student.

If you want good grades in a class, try not to miss more than two sessions a semester. Someone else's notes may help some, but they may actually harm you because you'll be mixing your interpretations and emphases with those of others. If you have to miss a class and use others' notes, it would be better to read several people's notebooks and talk with them about material that was presented in your absence. This is a much better way of digesting what was really said.

Another hint in keeping up with classes is the habit of avoiding procrastination. When work is assigned, begin it as soon as possible. Get extra reading out of the way and begin to work through your final outline. If more ideas occur to you, you may need to do some rewriting closer to deadline time. However, by getting work out of the way early, you not only eliminate one more pressure from your life; you also give yourself a feeling of success, having proven to yourself that you can keep up.

An important note here: school can be fun. It should also be educational. If you get your work done first, then there is always time to enjoy yourself without feelings of guilt or the false illusion that you are getting by.

The Paper Caper   What about all those research papers teachers assign with abandon? It seems no one can get through college without going through reams of typing or computer paper. Papers are as normal to college as icebergs are to the North Atlantic. One of the greatest helps you can give yourself is an understanding of them and an ability to do them quickly and well.

Once a general topic is assigned, decide what your exact topic will be. Some students spend days thinking about possible avenues of exploration, but really getting nowhere. Most instructors will assign a general area in which they want you to work. As long as your theme falls under the broad guidelines of what an instructor wants, you should be safe.

The best way to attack a paper is first to get a general idea, then visit the library. Be sure you don't just zero in on one or two books. Do some general reading until you become familiar with all the material available and useful to you. That, by the way, is one reason teachers assign papers! Once you are familiar enough with a subject, you can start a rough outline of how the paper might be developed, and then you're on your way.

Looking back at those books again, but now with some direction, you should be able to locate enough material so you can put some concrete concepts into your skeletal outline. After you've done some preliminary writing, you may realize the theme needs more development or some adjustment. Don't be afraid to do it, and don't panic. It happens all the time. You have enough work done by this time, so any changes shouldn't be catastrophic. Going back and rearranging your material shouldn't be too hard because you know enough about your subject to handle the changes. Some extra reading to fill in a gap or two should round out your paper.

Many students feel there is no way they can write a good paper. They may not have had much experience in writing while in high school, or they may feel inadequate with grammar, spelling, or technical writing ability. The best way to overcome any problems you have with papers is to understand that there is a systematic way of completing them easily and well. There is one little hitch, however. It will take some discipline on your part.

Young people are not famous for self-discipline. If you can make yourself get down to the business at hand and do it in a systematic way, working from the outline and information you have gathered, then completing the paper is a sure thing.

Once you can get the logistics and mechanical effort of a paper in hand, you can use your mind to actually absorb the material. This will not only help your grade, but your understanding of the material as well.

Another hint: don't use every big word you know or think you know. Professors are far more impressed by logical thinking than by an indiscriminate use of vocabulary. If you really understand what a word means and feel it's the right word for the right thought, by all means, use it. If, however, in your enthusiasm to impress the prof you decide to use words with which you are not familiar, you may actually hurt your chances for a good grade. When professors read papers in which words are misused, they quickly conclude that the students don't really grasp the concepts being presented. They may also assume those students haven't done enough outside reading and may therefore tend to give low grades on those papers.

If you know your writing skills are really weak, an elective course in basic grammar and composition would be well worth the extra time and money. It could boost your grades in college and serve you well later in life.

Flashing Blue Lights

Many professors, once you listen to them, have certain favorite areas of knowledge they like to stress. For example, an English teacher may consistently grade your writing low because you use verbs of being, and this person absolutely detests verbs of being! Once you understand that the instructor is adamant about such a point, you can do a lot to improve your theme grades simply by changing that one element in your writing.

It also helps to observe instructors. Notice their inflection as they speak. Many professors and teaching assistants, when they feel they are saying something important, will emphasize the point by speaking louder or more distinctly. They may use more hand motions and spend more time giving examples, perhaps even asking a few questions.

As you take notes, be sure to underline or color-code ideas, or somehow make a note to yourself that the teacher stressed this point. After you have attended a few classes, you should begin to see some pattern of material that this teacher considers important.

The most critical thing to remember as you begin your own class attack is to approach each course with a calm confidence that you will be able to do what is required of you. With a certain amount of discipline, a growing understanding of the teacher and his or her priorities, and a willingness to do the work, you shouldn't have to worry about doing poorly in any class.

Your time in the classroom can be one of tension, frustration, and almost uncontrollable fear, if you let that happen. On the other hand, it can be a time of growth and confidence if you are able to handle the material presented.

There will probably be people in each class who are more intelligent than you, but remember, everyone is experiencing the challenge, just as you are. Everyone will have to do the work, and everyone will have to discipline herself or himself to be interested, to ask questions, and to tackle the work assigned. If you can summon enough discipline to do that, you may just finish the course with a better grade than some of those geniuses who sit around you. Plus you surely will walk away from the class having done much to contribute to your real education—the growing process inside yourself.

Self-Check

1. How could you make better use of counselors and advisors?

   _____

   _____

2. What two things keep you from getting assignments done on time or from getting them done quickly, and how can you change these things?

   _____

   _____

3. What is the best way you study for tests? _____

   _____

4. How could you spend your study time better, both alone and in study groups?

   _____

   _____

Bridging the Gap

Teachers Need Study, Too

"You can't teach today's kids anything. Don't you realize they knew everything at birth?"

That's what one university professor says, and how you react to that comment is up to you.

An interesting phenomenon seems to be taking place with many college students today. With a few basic courses behind them, there are some who are more intent on using only that limited knowledge to do what they want, rather than wanting to learn more.

"I spend a lot of time arguing with students about how to get an assignment done," says another professor. "In the end, I feel I just waste time listening to them argue for their own mediocrity."

Teachers have one job—to educate. They are charged to make the Latin word *educare* work. *Educare* means "draw out," and that's what any good teacher wants to do with his or her students. To draw out the best an individual has, there must be a growing store of knowledge. Teachers want to draw out the best you have, not merely approve what you think you know already.

Reality Dose Number Two

You are the most important person in your college experience. The others who count most in your learning are not your parents, administrators, or even your friends. Instead, every teacher you have has special influence over you. To a great extent, your teachers will determine how successful you feel as a student as well as a person. They can provide you with much, or they can cause you extreme frustration. If you intend to get an education as well as maintain your sanity during these years, it would be in your best interest to learn how to deal with your instructors. In fact, it's essential.

A New Ball Game

Any poor attitude you have toward teachers may be a carryover from high school, and that's too bad. You must understand that the college situation doesn't put much emphasis on authority to make you learn, or get things done. Instead, college teachers leave students on their own and expect them to take care of and motivate themselves.

You are definitely on your own in college. People just expect you to do what's right or suffer the consequences. The decision to attend class, behave in an acceptable manner, or get an education is your responsibility. No one will come looking for you if you skip class. In fact, the only one you can play hooky on is yourself.

All this freedom and the new expectation of your maturity may be hard to accept at first. You may be accustomed to situations where others spoon-fed you or reminded you ten times to hand in an assignment. However, professors don't worry about things like that. They presume you have a sense of responsibility and know your obligations. Whether you choose to fulfill those obligations is totally up to you.

The professor-student relationship is an interesting one. There is a common goal, but college professors presume you will study or fail, and they feel justified in giving assignments. They allow you your own individuality and let you succeed or fall away by your own choice. That's a heavy responsibility.

If you still suffer from the high school attitude that teachers are your enemies, you have two choices. You can try to change that thinking, or resign yourself to a very bitter and miserable four years. Most professors truly do want you to learn.

Remember, teachers are also human. They'll have good and bad days, and they may not always understand when you're worrying about other things or when you just can't give them your undivided attention. They have pressures and problems just as you, and it may be wise to realize this before you judge them too harshly.

Their Humanity—Your Sanity

Professors, just like everyone else in this world, come in different sizes and mind-sets. Some will be open-minded, realistic individuals while others may be caught up in the narrowness of their isolated academic interests.

One of the best things you can do at the beginning of any class is to sit back and study the instructor. Before you start to jot down notes, take a good look at that individual. What is her or his body language saying? Does she or he seem relaxed and comfortable with you? Does the instructor fidget continuously and seem bored?

Listen to the prof's voice. Is it authoritative, strong, and rich with inflections and emphases? If so, you have found a person who is probably very strong in opinions and who expects a serious and attentive attitude from you. Here is a person who may be very busy and have little time to waste. As a result, the lectures will contain very little trivia. From her or his businesslike attitude, you can deduce that this teacher will expect the same from you.

You can't always judge professors by age, either. There are older instructors who are dynamic and very interested in you. They'll be alert and in tune with the times. Meanwhile, some younger professors you would expect to agree with your ideas and be more understanding of your pressures may be demanding and strict. They may be unsure of themselves or trying to prove their competence to administrators, and they'll try very hard to make your class, and you, a model of education.

Listening to a professor will give many clues to his or her priorities. Pay special attention to the examples the person gives; they'll often show another dimension of his or her life. Just remember that the best place to start in any class lies in studying the teachers. If you can begin to understand each of them, you'll know better how to study and prepare for their classes. You'll also learn more about human nature. You'll see adult traits you admire and would like to make your own, just as you'll see some undesirable characteristics. You can learn from these, too, by deciding you'll never permit yourself to let those traits become a part of you.

Facing Stereotypes

Remember the first page of this book? It advised you to step beyond the stereotypes of the "average" college student. Now the same advice prevails. Don't stereotype your teachers by age, looks, or teaching methods.

There, for example, is Professor A. He's really tough, almost to the point of regimentation. He gives tons of outside work, and the discipline in his class is absolutely absolute! He may be a little out of touch with the real world, but he means well, and he is offended if you don't think the material he's presenting is as important as he thinks it is. He teaches his subject because he totally believes in it. Professor A is a member of the "old guard." He may have been a sergeant in the army, or at least he may give that impression. In his class, excuses never will go far.

On the other hand, young Professor B is a member of the "new guard." She got her education at a large university and considers herself fairly liberal. She's a great lover of human nature, and she detests not ignorance itself, but those who choose to remain ignorant. She'll be open and usually will give you a hearing when you come with questions. Some professors of this type tend to be taken advantage of by students who appeal to their sense of justice and fair play, and that's unfortunate. These instructors are willing to give you the benefit of a doubt, if they are taken advantage of too often, they may tend to back off into a more unbending attitude toward everyone. They are good people and shouldn't be abused because of their willingness to try to understand and make allowances.

What we might call the "modern guard" of professors are the instructors who are in tune with the times and who are not afraid to get off the track once in a while. They believe not all education can be planned and that part of it must evolve from the current needs and questions of the class. These people are not easily fooled because they are aware of the tricks students use. They may even have used a few themselves in their own college days!

What is the best way to deal with the modern guard? Be honest and be yourself. Don't bother trying to set up a facade for these people. They can see right through you, and they'll be insulted if you try to deal with them in less than an honest way. Being open is the best way to win their admiration and cause them to develop a genuine interest in you. They usually will be understanding and considerate. However, they will expect you to have your priorities straight and assume you are willing to be taught.

Interested People are Interesting People

Even if you are in a large lecture class, the key to your success in that course lies in asking questions.

Of course there are six million arguments for explaining why you may not ask questions, ranging from a weak voice to excuses like "I don't want to seem dumb in front of others" or "I don't want to seem like I'm playing up to the professor." There are students who do play up to teachers, and there are intellectual snobs here and there. These people are usually easy to spot, and the kind of questions they ask is not what is being discussed here. If you ask honest, intelligent questions, this will almost ensure you a good grade, simply because it takes a basic understanding of the lecture to ask an intelligent question. People who don't know anything never ask questions. They don't understand enough.

Most professors are in the classroom to teach. There is not a professor in the world who doesn't appreciate the student who will raise a hand occasionally and ask a question that shows familiarity with the material. Besides, most teachers get tired of hearing only their own voices all the time!

By asking questions you also can keep the professor motivated. There are many teachers who sense the decline in esteem for their profession, and you can be sure you are not the first person to hear a certain instructor's lecture. If no one asks questions, all you will get from that person is the same stock lecture he or she may have delivered for years. However, if you stop the lecture periodically and ask for more information, you can make the teacher dig deeper into his or her experience and knowledge. Then the teacher will come up with little sidelines and extra bits of knowledge that make the material more understandable and memorable. These are the things that often help when you're trying to grasp a particular problem. Let another human voice sound through that classroom and see what happens. The instructor will not only notice you and be aware of your interest, but other students will realize how important a good question can be to change the pace of a lecture, and they'll join in, too.

Find the Real Enemy   Your teachers are sincere about your education, and most of them are behind the desk or podium to do a good job. Just remember that they are human, and they'll have their bad days, too. Respect their knowledge. Try to understand their uniqueness, and give them an opportunity to be aware of you as an individual who is really trying to get something out of their classes.

You don't have to be on opposite sides of a confrontation. You are not enemies. The real enemy is ignorance, and if you and your teachers can work together, you will both succeed in the goal you have in common—real education. Give it a try!

Self-Check   1. Describe how your attitude toward teachers has changed from elementary, through high school, and into the present. Has it improved or deteriorated?

_____

_____

2. What keeps you from asking questions in class, and what steps can you take to overcome those things?

_____

3. Who is the most ineffective teacher you have, and what makes that person that way?

_____

How can you get that person to be more effective? _____

_____

4. If you were a teacher, how would you rate *your* performance in the classroom?

_____

5. How would you describe the ideal teacher?

_____

_____

It's Called Studying | 10

The Lively Art of Self-Improvement

What are some of the most solitary things you can do? Read? Listen to music? Write letters?

One of the most solitary things, in addition to long-distance running, has to be studying. There are times when, no matter what mood you're in, certain work has to be done. Chapters of books have to be read and absorbed. Papers must be tackled. Or just some plain, hard studying needs to be done. Procrastination can't last forever, especially when you have a test scheduled for the next afternoon! A deadline for a paper is simply that—you may get to that line half-dead, but you will be under the wire!

You Against the World

Studying is hard work. There's no getting around that fact. One of the most difficult things you can ever ask yourself to do is sit down, block out all the people and things that usually claim much of your attention—and concentrate.

If you are going to succeed in college, one thing you'll have to understand is that somehow, sometimes, you will have to be able to isolate yourself and study. All the paper in the world, extra work, questions in class, and anything else you can think of won't help if you don't do the basic work of studying the material presented.

There is a possibility you are still at a point in your life where you feel you don't have the discipline required for honest study. If so, you may consider "stopping out" of school for a semester or a year until you get your act together.

One of the hardest facts of life you may need to comprehend now is that no one can make you study, just as no one can make you succeed. Maturity is living one's own life, and disciplining one's self enough to work toward desired goals. If you don't have what it takes in that department, you need to sit yourself down and give yourself the most difficult lecture you can hear. Or you can refuse to develop the focus and self-discipline you need to succeed in college. In that case you might as well stop reading this book and forget about college—at least until your attitude improves.

Future employers will expect you to keep learning—from manuals and seminars. Make sure your study habits will not disappoint them.

What's Noteworthy?

Notes are extremely important for study. In high school, your teachers may have emphasized neatness in notebooks and even collected them from time to time to make sure you were on top of the material and had it well organized.

College isn't like that. Put into your notes whatever will help you understand or emphasize a certain point the teacher makes during a lecture. Draw, diagram, doodle. Invent your own shorthand. For extra help, take time to review your notes soon after each class. At that time, reorganize the material and highlight—perhaps with colored pens—key points and the most important information you need to remember.

Good note taking is a must in college. Your notes will contain more for your practical knowledge than your textbooks will because they show your understanding of the material, as well as what the teacher stressed. Textbooks are supplementary. They're useful, and they can help supply the background and resource material of what you've learned in class. Your notes remain all-important.

If you're one of those people whose notes consist of various pieces of paper stuck into different books, jean pockets, or jackets, you may be in trouble. A good notebook or folder where you can keep all the material for one course together is an excellent investment. When you are ready to study, everything will be available, and with some good outlining, it should be fairly easy to follow and understand.

You notes are for *you*. Don't worry about what anyone else thinks. They may not see the need for that art scribbled in the margins, or they may not like the arrows, different colors, or various methods of emphasizing things. If *you* can understand them, your notes are doing the job they're meant to do.

With good notes in hand, half the battle is won when it comes to study time. Now, how do you study?

Get Out of Your Room

Studying, because it demands so much from you, may require some minor adjustments in your life as well as in your head. Many college students try to study in their rooms, but this isn't always the best place. Your room is where you live and where, usually, others visit or live with you. If you can get away to the library, to a quiet part of the student union, or to some out-of-the-way lounge or unused room, you'll find that studying becomes easier. Some dorms even provide study areas. Find out if there is anything like this available, and use it. Many distractions you found in your room won't be there, and it will make going back to where you live a lot nicer.

Once you have your notes in hand, the best way to study is to read over a certain section quickly to get a general idea of the material. Then go back and systematically review, emphasizing key points and, if necessary, underlining again. Using memory tricks such as first words of sentences can help with some material, but your real understanding will come when you try explaining what you know to someone else.

Once you've done as much as you can by yourself, it may not be a bad idea to review with someone else from your class. If you discuss problems or hazy areas together, both of you will gain new insights into what the teacher said. Even if you have to help the other person, consider it an investment in your own education. You'll never learn anything better than when you have to explain it to someone else until that person understands it.

The Group   Not a bunch of rock stars or part of the old neighborhood, the study group is one of the wisest collections of people in the world, if that is why they come together—to study. In order to make a study group work, however, some guidelines must be set and met.

For example, if you and a few classmates get together to study and the time quickly deteriorates into a social hour or gripe session, the purpose of the group is destroyed and you all are wasting your time. A study group also demands that each person pull his or her own weight, and this involves a certain amount of preparation on everyone's part before the group meets. If a few people are doing all the work and the rest are just hangers-on, the group won't last very long. Those who come and simply listen, hoping they'll hear enough to help them pass a course, are being unfair. As long as they're around, the group will never succeed. People who simply want private tutors should hire them. Study groups are for sharing.

Find a few people, and only a *few* people, who share your same interest in a class and who are willing to work. Meet occasionally in a comfortable place where there are limited distractions, and you'll find such sessions valuable.

Most students don't need study groups for every class. Only the difficult or advanced courses may require a group to meet throughout the entire semester. For example, medical and law students often share their notes and study together because the material they are required to know is often complicated and overwhelming.

A lot more study groups come into existence around exam time. As the end of a semester nears, it's a good idea to find some people and study together a few times. If you've done your homework with the text and your notes, study groups can benefit everyone, clarifying the material and putting the entire course into perspective. Just remember, if study groups are to succeed, they should be set for a definite, limited time, and the people involved should come prepared.

Study as much as possible on your own. Have notes that are decipherable and right for you. Then look around and see if anyone is willing to discuss the material with you. If you can make a study group work, the experience can be rewarding in many ways. You may even gain a few friends out of it. Sharing knowledge is always better than keeping it bottled up inside you, and it's a great way to begin any new friendship. Learning to work meaningfully with others will also be a valuable tool when you are out in the career of your choice.

Cracking the Books without Cracking Up

One thing you have in common with many adults in today's society is the amount of stress you must endure. College puts some intense demands on students, especially in some subject areas. If you are serious about your education and you need to learn certain things to fulfill your dreams for a career, you may feel deluged by the amount of material you are required to learn. Stress has almost become as common in today's world as a cold or the flu. However, it is a lot harder to overcome. Some colleges even offer electives or seminars on pressures dealing with college life. Look into them if you feel the need.

The biggest key as you fight stress, however, is not to overdo anything. Start overcoming some of the trademarks of youth! Don't overdo study, and don't overdo the party scene. No one wants you to have a nervous breakdown, but it may be up to you to make sure such a thing doesn't happen.

Much of the pressure you feel comes from the importance of preparing for the future. In many circumstances, it isn't enough to pass a course. You may need a certain score or test average to qualify for advanced classes. Students who are planning to continue in demanding fields know they must score high enough to win acceptance into specialized and highly competitive training programs.

For many, this is the first time this kind of pressure has been felt. Before it was enough just to pass and move on. Knowing you must score higher than many other qualified students may put unreal pressure on you, forcing you to study longer and do more extra work than teachers require. Only you can decide how much study is important. Only you know when that study time has ceased to be profitable and has deteriorated into a matter of simply cracking the books, forcing your mind to concentrate.

Most stress management programs present techniques for overcoming pressure to their counselees. "Video wallpaper," a television movie of a relaxing scene such as a shoreline or a wheat field waving in the wind, has been used with some effectiveness. Just imagining such scenes works for a lot of people. Soothing music also helps some. Getting off for a walk around campus may also help. Only you know what relaxes you and eases tension. Also, only you can make sure that there is time enough each week to do it.

If sports, by their physical exertion, make you forget your pressures, use them. A good game of tennis or racquetball can leave you physically exhausted, and when your body is tired, your mind also has a chance to relax.

Don't be one of those people who stays cooped up for hours, never getting any physical exercise and wondering why you feel listless and nervous. Find activities that release pressure for you, then do them. Jog, bike, get enough sleep, and arrange some relaxing evenings with good friends. Get involved with local sports or workout clubs, and make use of the gym or swimming pool, if you like this kind of activity. Also take advantage of the many good movies that are shown free or for a minimal charge on campus.

Go ahead. Do all that studying you need to do. Give it your best shot, and try to be as disciplined and as organized as possible. Then do something, whatever it is, to make yourself relax. You owe it to the rest of the world, and you owe it most of all to yourself!

Self-Check

1. What are the greatest flaws in your study habits, and can how you overcome them?

_____

_____

2. Name two places where you can study without major disruption, and how often you can get to them.

_____

_____

3. Name three relaxations you use regularly to relieve stress.

_____

_____

4. What or who is your biggest distraction, and how can you overcome it?

_____

_____

5. What was your best study experience, and what did it involve?

_____

_____

Tools of the Trade

Getting By with a Little Help

Some people spend hundreds of dollars for equipment; some professionals spend thousands. The artist takes great care of prized brushes, and the writer considers some pens and even a computer semisacred items.

Your job right now is to allow yourself to be educated, and just as there are tools of the trade for any profession, there are tools for this temporary career called college.

What you do with the money available to you is your business. Just remember, college is your business right now, but there may be times when you have some options. You don't have to buy every gimmick you can find. A short list of priority items can do the job, and they are what you should concentrate on securing.

Just My Type   One common question for incoming freshmen is, "Do I need a computer? Do I need a word processor or a typewriter?"

The answer is yes, but you'll need to determine your special needs. If, for example, you're taking classes which need extensive figuring and complicated work, then a computer will be necessary, even though it is a highly expensive item. Your school has computer labs available for students, and making good use of them may be one way out of having to buy a computer yourself.

Most college courses can be fulfilled with a simple word processor or a typewriter. The one item you'll find yourself needing and saving for is a word processor, because it is faster and allows for easier and quicker editing than a typewriter. If the funds aren't there now for one, consider channeling some of your other expenses into the frugal column. A word processor will not only serve you well during these college years, it also will be a valuable tool in the years ahead. Most professors demand that work be presented in a typed format (which can be accomplished with a good-quality printer on a word processor) so this item is a worthwhile investment. If you truly can't afford a word processor or typewriter of your own, you may be able to rent one for a few hours at a time at the library at rates comparable to photocopying.

Most people have gained at least limited skill in keyboarding by the time they reach college. If you haven't, take some time out in the local computer lab and practice. Just as driving a car often is necessary in today's world, a working ability to move around those three rows of keys also is a necessary skill. Rather than use the old "biblical" method, "Seek and ye shall find," get a keyboarding book and make yourself learn where the letters are. It's not that difficult, and most people who have trouble typing do so because of mental blocks, not ineptitude. If you think extra attention from a professional would help, enroll in a basic typing or keyboarding class. The skills you learn will come in handy well beyond your college years.

"This Is a   What about taping lectures? Too hard, you say. Never
Recording..."   enough time to play it all back. Bingo! Taping every lecture not only gives you a false sense of having the material available, it also is simply an unworkable excuse for not taking good notes and engaging in honest study.

Tape recorders are no substitute for listening, but they

can be valuable tools. For example, if a teacher is reviewing an entire unit of work, it could be useful to tape that lecture.

A better use for a recorder comes *after* you have studied certain material. In a quiet place, talk for five or ten minutes about key points and insights and make an outline of the material you've reviewed. When exam time rolls around, it will be much easier to listen to your short tapes made after concentrated study, and it will give you a solid based for semester finals.

Getting used to your own voice on tape may be slightly traumatic at first, but once you are comfortable, you may even find your speech and diction improving, since you'll be more aware of how you sound to others. That could help boost your confidence level, too.

Odds and Ends   Having the right equipment does more than make your job easier. It also gives you a sense of being organized and prepared for work. Consider your notebooks, pens, pencils, and other equipment part of your wealth right now.

Your books were a major expense and deserve special treatment. Choosing to keep some after college will give you another reason for highlighting and making notes in their margins. You may refer back to some of these books years from now, and you'll then appreciate the attentiveness you gave them.

A good set of markers and highlighters is an inexpensive but necessary item. Colored markers are probably the best way to organize notes. You can make certain material stand out immediately by using different colors, and you can coordinate notes into general areas or emphasize certain specifics that are really ''red letter!''

Several good notebooks and a supply of paper may seem trivial, but it can save you time when time is extremely precious. If you are one of those people who must run to the bookstore every time you turn around, your lack of organization may do more than waste time. It also may give you a feeling of never quite being caught up with the business of performing like a student.

Notebooks and folders, in which you keep each set of course notes organized, should become a little library in your room. Set them off with bookends so you know you can put your hands on any specific material whenever you need it. Organization is as important to getting things done as discipline is to making room for study time.

You may feel the right equipment is unnecessary, but no team ever takes the field without it. College, with its demands, requires that you give yourself every help you can.

Whatever your subject area, be prepared for it, and you'll find that class becomes a lot easier when you have what you need and are prepared. Very often a professional's tools become some of his or her most cherished items. You may not exactly become wild about your word processor, but it can become something with which you associate accomplishment and success. Give it a chance.

Self-Check

1. How much of your monthly budget do you spend on learning-related material? _____ What does this say about your present priorities?

   _____

   _____

2. Do you expect your parents to pay for learning material? If you do, what does this say about you? Is it your education or theirs?

   _____

   _____

3. If someone asked you to collect all your notes for a certain class right now, could you do it? _____ What could help you be more organized in note taking and compiling specific material for a certain course?

   _____

   _____

4. Name the three most important items dedicated to your education right now.

   _____

   _____

   _____

5. Name three priorities in your spending allowance, and give yourself an honest reason for allowing them such importance.

_____

_____

_____

Getting Involved

Is It Worth the Price?

Given the fact that there are loners and there are joiners, something must be said about making the most of your college years. High school had its different kinds of people, but in one category there were only two groups. There were those who got involved in extracurricular activities such as sports, journalism, drama, or music. Then there were those who left school so fast every day that the bell was still echoing through the halls as their jackets swished through the doors.

Whether or not you were involved in activities during high school, college presents a different picture. There are many more opportunities available now because there are so many new and different kinds of people with diverse interests.

How much you get out of college, as with everything else, depends on how much you put into it. Clubs, organizations, and special interest groups may take up a lot of extra time, but if they give you the opportunity for meeting new people and broadening your horizons, they are worth the extra hours. You'll find that whatever career you are pursuing has its own branches of career-affiliated organizations on campus. They will not only give you a chance for hands-on experience in your field, but will add to that first real resume as well. Activities such as working on the college newspaper may even pay a small salary or give you college credit for in-service training.

Very often when a young person applies for that first real job, personnel representatives will be much more interested in the applicant's actual working experience in the field than in class rank or how many credit hours were taken per semester. They realize that no matter how many courses an individual takes, that person still needs a certain amount of training in the practical realities of actually doing the job with others who are mature, responsible workers.

Join the Club!

There are many organizations on campus that merit your consideration. Some are geared to political activity, while others espouse certain causes or ideals. You may have to look for them because many organizations don't advertise themselves enough, but they are worth finding. These groups are often very specialized, and the people involved don't always have time to put up posters in every hall or on every bulletin board. It would be worth it to look around and see what's available, especially if you are new to your school as a freshman or a transfer student.

Even if you have been in college a year or two, there are always new clubs and organizations springing up. Keep your eyes and ears open for these, and consider getting involved with a group that may hold some interest for you. Very often the side interests that were developed in college lead to career possibilities, or at least into some enjoyable leisure activities in adulthood. Political involvement, drama, or special-interest clubs can offer a lot both now and later on.

Sport—Not Supersport

You may be involved with a varsity team in your school, though chances are you are probably not. Does this mean all sporting activities are closed to you?

The athletes who may be in school on athletic scholarships and who view their college play as a stepping-stone to professional sports are very serious about their work. They plan on careers in this area and therefore approach training and playing as diligently as others tackle their classes.

Most students, however, can take advantage of intramural programs or just a friendly game of frisbee, tennis, or touch football out behind the dorm. And in cases such as these, there's little pressure. It's just some good, friendly enjoyment and exercise.

Physical activity, whether it be jogging or playing organized sports, is healthy and helps clear the mind to prepare for some good, hard study. The "fun" college sports carry with them no great tension. Participation in the fun sports is also a great outlet for pent-up energy.

A good workout in the gym or swimming pool, or just a bike ride around campus, are some activities that can be as much a part of your day as study time and meals. You don't have to be a supersport to enjoy sports; you just have to be human.

Who's Running This Place?

Another area in which you may consider becoming involved is your student government. Since administrators in college are so removed from you and everyday situations, there is much more opportunity for students to be effective in decision-making situations. Your high school may have had a good student council where some of the opinions expressed actually made it to the principal's office. If so, you were lucky. Most high schools allow very little room for student participation when it comes to developing rules.

Student government in college is different. It often makes many of the laws that govern life on campus and in the individual dorms. When it speaks to the school administration, it usually is listened to because most deans and administrators are genuinely interested in what students feel will help things work more smoothly. Student government will take some of your free time, but it's a good way to get some exposure to the decision-making process. It can make you a much more effective parent when your own children are in school, and it can be a springboard for civic involvement, participation in politics, or getting involved in your company's management process later on.

Maybe you have never been involved in student government before. Maybe you never considered the possibility. Consider it now. If you're willing to spend the time, you can meet new people who are real leaders, and you can get involved in a meaningful way. Exercising a certain amount of leadership in college is one of the best things you can do for yourself. It gives you a feeling of being able to handle things and being a success in dealing with people, both as one in authority and as one who must deal with higher authority. It demands initiative and a certain amount of creatvity, but it's worth the effort. Think about it.

Build Some Good Memories

College life is very complicated and can make you tense, if you let it. By getting involved in some of the enjoyable activities on campus, you can develop a healthier attitude toward school in general and enjoy yourself in the process.

The big help that getting involved in activities will give you is the chance to be with people who share your values in a meaningful yet relaxed way. The days of spending your time with only a few close friends should be behind you. There are so many people on any college campus that it's almost impossible not to find some individuals who can make your life more interesting and help you enjoy your years in school more. All you have to do is get out of your room once in a while and look!

It's true there is a price you pay for getting involved. And that price—at a time in your life when there aren't enough hours in the day to do everything you feel necessary—may be too high if you're not careful. You may need to see your life in a different perspective, even now as you move through college. You want to get a good education. You want to succeed. You also want to develop yourself as a person and give yourself every opportunity to meet new friends. You need new experiences that can add to your fullness as a person later on. Giving up some of your precious time is a price worth paying for all of that!

Many of the memories and good experiences you'll carry with you into adult life will not come from classes or the time you spend in the library poring over research material. It is the people and the enjoyable times, the memorable hours and the extra effort you spend in some activity or project that will impress you the most and provide some of your best memories of college. Give yourself a chance to build those memories. You'll never regret it.

Self-Check   1. What are the reasons many people don't bother to get involved in activities in college, and how can those reasons be addressed?

_____

_____

2. Name three interests you have that might find outlet in some activities on or near the campus.

_____

_____

_____

3. What is your attitude toward student government? What could you offer it?

_____

_____

The Commuter College

13

Is It the Best of Both Worlds?

The commuter college has been around a long time. Now more than ever, it has become the school of choice for a growing number of students. If money is a problem or family circumstances demand that a son or daughter stay home a few more years, the commuter college is a place where the young person can get an education without totally disappearing from the family scene. It's much cheaper, but it also carries some unique problems because of its special circumstances.

Most students who go to school locally find themselves in a constant three-way split between home, school, and the part-time job they usually hold. Because of this, many young people who attend commuter schools may get the feeling they are not really in college, but they couldn't be farther from the truth.

School is school, and those who attend commuter schools are often misled because they don't "go away" to a large campus. Sprawling buildings do not necessarily make a particular school any better than others. Good teachers are also found in commuter schools, and they often have the extra dimension of running their own businesses or working part-time in their fields of expertise. As a result, they offer more than book knowledge. They speak from past and current experience, and they can be real leaders and role models to their students.

The very fact that commuter college students are going to school while trying to honor commitments at home and hold jobs on the side shows they are serious about education. There have been, and there still are, students who go away to a college campus not particularly to get an education or to prepare themselves for careers, but simply to avoid the realities of adult life for a few more years. Life becomes very demanding for the young person who is willing to make the sacrifices and constant adjustments necessary to stay in school as well as keep all the other facets of life functioning well in his or her hometown.

Split-Level Problems

One of the greatest areas that may cause concern if you are a commuter student is your life at home. You may live in a split-level house. Nonetheless, no matter what your home looks like, if you live at home you either are—or will soon be—aware of changes that have occurred between you and each of your family members. Your folks may be trying to give you more freedom and may be honoring your sense of independence. The fact remains, though, that you are still under their roof, and often severe conflicts can arise when college students, knowing others their age are off and on their own, feel the tension of still obeying certain family rules. They sometimes can become bitter because of obligations that exist because they are still at home—still a day-to-day part of the family, with needs and demands of its own. Total freedom is simply not there, and though you may be trying to assert your individuality as a young adult, the very fact that you go home every night to the people who governed your childhood makes maturity that much harder to claim.

What can you do?

Some good, honest discussion with your folks is a necessity if you intend to survive and make the most of your commuter situation. Your parents may not realize you are as mature as you are, and as a result, they may need help understanding some basic facts of your life.

Arguing or trying to assert your independence from the family in a negative way only causes tension and trouble. Younger brothers and sisters may already resent the freedom you have and complain about it to your parents, making things even harder for you. On the other hand, your folks, wanting to give you freedom but also striving to keep the family unit on an even keel, may make certain demands you may feel are unreasonable at this stage of your development.

You may not be the type who can hold up at a summit conference at home, but finding a quiet, relaxed time to talk to your parents about your situation will help. Fighting for freedom at home never works, but proving your maturity and willingness to help as much as you can usually makes parents more receptive to your desires and will probably get you that additional freedom you crave.

Some commuter students also experience another kind of frustration on the home front. Because they may work and have school assignments, they can't spend time with the family as much as some would wish. The only way to overcome commuter student problems is with honest discussion and by a realistic facing of all sides of the situation. If you commute to school, you know you don't have as much time as you had in high school. Your class schedule probably changes with the various days of the week, and keeping up with the flexible hours in your work schedule puts time you spend at home at even more of a premium.

What you can do is try to improve the quality of time you do spend at home. You don't need to be present in the family room for an entire evening to convey to family members that you still care about them, and still consider them a precious part of your life.

It's true that going to school while still living at home demands some adjustment to your thinking. Nevertheless, once you can realize it is possible to care about both situations and give to both, you should be able to work out a reasonable amount of success on both fronts. Hopefully, everyone in your family wants you to succeed. With a little help from you, they can learn to understand the pressures you feel from all those different areas in your life.

Succeeding in college doesn't mean just getting a diploma. It also means succeeding as a human being who has acquired a particular set of skills and a certain amount of knowledge. By living at home, you have the opportunity to let your family watch your daily growth toward adulthood for a few years longer than other families can. Let them see the good things that are happening to you, and try to share enough of your life with them so that both you and they can feel you are growing.

Out On Your Own? Living at home offers many advantages for commuter students. It is less expensive and allows students to maintain contact with their families and ease the transition from high school to college life.

But living at home is not a requirement for commuter students, and for some it may not be a workable solution. You may find it too distracting to study at home while your younger sister or brother is watching television or entertaining friends. You may find that you and your parent or parents are not able to negotiate reasonable compromises that allow you the freedom you need.

What to do?

If you find you can afford it, getting an apartment with another student may be the answer. It will allow you to have more control over your surroundings, and it may well ease the tension between you and other family members. Living on your own is also good practice for those who intend to finish their degrees at a larger school.

Just be sure you make the decision to move out for the right reasons, and be sure living on your own really fits into your budget. You should be sure before you move that you've made a good faith effort to resolve your problems at home, and you should understand that those problems won't go away without work just because you have your own place.

Make It Work Some commuter students wrongly feel they really don't belong to their college. Since they come to campus and leave, usually quite quickly, there is the danger of feeling like an outsider. Inasmuch as all commuter colleges deal with people who are living at home—who are close to old friends and who are trying to hold down jobs at the same time—there also may be a tendency to be less congenial with other students. This leads to a comment made by commuter students when visiting a large school away from home. "It's so different down here," one said. "Everyone seems much more willing to stop and talk!"

The reason for this is because, on some other campuses, *everyone* is away from home and old friends. Everyone who goes away to school has left a great part of his or her life behind and therefore feels the need to develop new friends and different contacts. As a result, distant campuses tend to be friendlier places because students have learned very quickly that they need each other.

What can the commuter student do?

First, try to break down some walls and let others know you're ready for conversation and sharing of ideas. Since commuter students are often in a hurry after class to rush off to another part of their lives, it may be harder to find individuals with time to talk. There will be those situations, however, when students are in the lounge, bookstore, or snack shop. A warm look in your eyes and a smile on your face will let others know you are a person who can be approached and who is willing to share.

Another way to break down any isolation you may feel within your commuter college is by getting involved with activities within the school. True, there is that old problem of time, but there are areas where you could become involved if you wanted to. Student government, school publications, organizations, clubs, and special interest groups all exist, just as they do on a large campus. You'll find that the students involved in them are usually exceptional people, the type of leaders who have learned how to balance their time and fit other activities into an already busy day. They will also be the people who will, in later life, be the doers, the initiators, and the motivators. They don't look for excuses or use difficult situations as a reason for doing nothing. They see a situation that interests them, make time for it, and then act. Very often those who were involved in commuter college activities go on to become active in the larger community, and with the network of former classmates to draw from, they can make a positive and powerful impact.

If you are a commuter student and feel lonely because of the lack of good friends at school, investigate some of the programs available and let others know you are willing to communicate. If you don't get involved in some activity at school, you may never feel you really belong. It may take more effort on your part, and people may seem too busy to give you the time you feel you need. However, rather than give up and stay in your own shell, you can try getting involved and meeting others who share your interests.

In a commuter school there will also be a great temptation to hang on to your old high school friends and avoid making new ones. Fight that temptation. There are too many good people on campus. It would be a real waste not to get to know them and let them become aware of you. You don't have to drop any of your old friends who are now part of the commuter college scene with you, but don't limit yourself to your old social patterns. Part of college should involve expanding your experience and your expectations of yourself. It may take some new people around you to make that happen. Don't be afraid to let them in.

Commuter schools often have students of various ages enrolled. Take advantage of this and learn to pick the brains of older persons who are on your level of class work but who have a lot more experience in the school of living. They can teach you much over a cup of coffee or waiting for classes to start. Make room for them in your life, and you'll find they can add an entirely new and rich dimension to your college experience.

Striking a Balance

Many young people today attend a local branch of a major university for the first year or two, then go to the main campus to finish their college careers. Money problems often dictate this kind of split-level college life, and while it is sometimes difficult, it is rarely impossible to handle.

While at the local school, some students yearn for the days when they'll be leaving home. If you find yourself in this situation, don't spend all your time dreaming of life on campus, thinking things will be fantastically better than they are now.

True, you will be away from your parents' influence, and that may take several weeks or months of adjustment, but why bother living in the future when your present can be so exciting? Use your time well in the school where you are, and if you feel trapped by family pressures at home, be a giving, caring member of that family while you are still there. Seeing this, others may learn to care more, too.

If you can learn to tackle the college situation, however it exists in your life, you'll be far ahead of those students who may have run away from home to school and who are just fending off the adult world for a few more years. By learning to balance your time between home, school, and work, you not only get an education to match the best of them and keep a good relationship with your family, you also can learn to manage your life in a way that others may never quite be able to attain.

Holding Up While Holding a Job

Most young people who attend local colleges usually also hold part-time jobs. There are even times when that job starts eating into other areas such as study time, family commitments, and social life. Money continues to be one of the essential commodities in our world. It's needed so you can pay for your education just as it is also needed in so many other areas of life. Money, however, and the need for it, can get to be a problem when that part-time job interferes too much with the more important areas of your life and with your hopes for the future.

Many parents, knowing their sons and daughters are staying home for college, expect them to get jobs. In many homes that is just a simple necessity. Parents also feel there are certain hours of the day that are expendable. Often they don't know how much study time you need because they don't know your work load. As a result, they may feel their college-aged offspring still need to contribute something, if not to the rest of the family, at least to their own financial needs.

You may be under tremendous pressure to help put food on the family table or to pay your own way through school. This is becoming more common as the financial situation of many families grows more and more strained. It should also make you more determined than ever to stay in school and learn the skills of today, preparing for the more technical skills of tomorrow the very best you can.

You also have your own financial needs, such as clothes, some entertainment, and other things you feel are important. The problem in this case is to keep everything in the proper perspective. When you were younger, you may have spent the largest part of your budget on entertainment and junk food. With realistic needs coming home to roost, you may need to rethink how much money it really takes to feed your own pleasure. The adult world usually puts its own pleasure much farther down in the spending list. That is because it is aware of commitments to children, job expenses, and the cost of merely living and commuting to work. When the adult is the person who has to pay all the bills, suddenly entertainment falls farther down the list of necessities, and adults learn to make their own entertainment on a much smaller budget.

If your need for money is so great that you must work longer hours than are reasonable for your life right now, consider working full-time for a semester or a year to save enough to enable you later to go to school and give your class demands the time they deserve.

Trying to get the most out of college if you are exhausted from the job that is paying for that education really doesn't make much sense. Study isn't easy, and it demands your best effort. If you increasingly find your best energy and all your strength going into your job—if you find yourself putting in more hours as the weeks go on, and if you are allowing your boss to call you in when you know you should be studying or need time for yourself—you may be making money that you'll wind up spending on doctors' bills and ulcer medicine. Also, you will be wasting your opportunity to get the most your college courses have to offer.

If it takes a family discussion to get out your feelings about time, job, school, and home, by all means have that discussion. As long as it is done in a quiet and informative way, it will be a positive thing. It is possible to work and even to enjoy some of those hours of employment while still making the most of other parts of your life, but only you can decide how much time you realistically can put into your part-time job and still keep up with school demands. Only you know how much of your time and presence is needed at home and how much attention you'll have to give family members.

If you work, make sure that your job stays in its rightful place in your life right now. Be sure it is not sapping most of your energy. The reason you're in college is presumably to get a better job with a more optimistic future. If you spend too much time working at a menial job that will probably lead nowhere, you may be depriving yourself of the chance to learn enough from your classes to get that good position later on.

Money is important. That's a fact of life. But it's not nearly as important as you, your sanity, your sense of being on top of your own life, and the possibilities your future holds. Go ahead and hold that job. Just make sure it doesn't have a stranglehold on you!

Self-Check   1. If you are a commuting student, do you have any negative attitudes toward your present way of attending college?

_____

_____

2. What can you do in your present situation to overcome some of those feelings?

_____

3. Describe your current relationship with family members. Is it better or worse since you started attending college locally, and why?

_____

_____

4. What could ease some of the tension of time, job, and family in your life right now and how can you make it happen?

_____

_____

_____

5. What part of your life is getting the lion's share of time right now?

_____

6. What does this say about the quality of your life, and is it a good thing?

_____

_____

7. On a scale of 1–10, with 10 being the highest, how would you rate your ability to live in the split-level world of home, college, and a job? _____

_____

What one thing would make it easier and less stressful for you, and how can you make that happen?

_____

_____

COPING AND CONQUERING

Part III

The Money Crunch

14

How Big a Bite?   Money has always been a problem. No matter how much you have, it seems you could always use a little more. Belonging to a sorority or fraternity, for example, can be quite an additional expense.

It is almost inevitable that the cost of education will continue to spiral upward, and you may feel you are being priced out of the opportunity for a good education. This isn't necessarily so.

Because college costs are rising, more financial aid is available from a number of different sources. In fact, new scholarships are being instituted almost every year. If you have never looked into the possibilities for aid, it may be worth your while to see if you and your family qualify for financial aid under the Basic Educational Opportunity Grant Program. Money is awarded through this program on the basis of college costs as well as family income, and this may be important for choosing the school you wish to attend. Or, if you are considering moving to another school and that college has higher costs, you could still consider the change realistically, knowing your money from the program would increase as your college costs increase.

Although you may not be getting financial aid now, conditions at home and in government standards have gone through some recent changes. Thus, you may be eligible for help without even knowing it. Also, if you are already in college, you might check with the school and the financial aid office. There are too many students already in college or well near the end of their college years who find out too late that money was available to them, but they were never informed of it. Many high school counselors are overworked, and some may not know of all the monies available to you in your particular school, with your particular line of study, and with the ethnic, working, and social background of your family. No matter where you are in your college career, take the time to investigate money available to you now. Laws may have changed. Your family's income may have changed. At the least, you'll be confident that you have covered every avenue open to you to make sure you have the chance to get all the financial help you can.

Some Rich Resources

The first place you can find help in financial areas, as well as with other things, is with your college counselor or adviser. He or she can help you get the necessary information from the College Scholarship Service, a nationwide organization. Most important, though, is the fact that your counselor will know you are in the market for financial help. If he or she does not have the necessary information for your particular needs, a collective search for more aid for you will be undertaken. Your counselor will also, at your request, consult others in the financial office about the possibility of more aid. Don't be afraid to use this help. Too many young people feel they must make it through school on their own or just with their parents' help. They fail to check into the many programs that offer financial assistance and end up making it unnecessarily hard on themselves.

Your college or university has many financial loans and grants, and there are agencies and many businesses that provide scholarships. There are also many private sources for money, and these are all possibilities for extra revenue as you continue your schooling. It pays to check into all of them.

For example, where are your parents employed? Are there any scholarships or partial grants available through these companies? Is one of your parents deceased? There may be money through his or her past employer available to you. Has someone else failed to honor a scholarship, leaving you the opportunity to pick it up halfway through your own college career? There are also assistance programs and loans, and if you are not aware of all the possibilities for additional monies in your school, go see your counselor.

There is money available if you need it, but you'll have to initiate the investigation of all possible sources, and then you'll have to get the applications in before specific deadlines. Many college students fail to qualify for money that is easily attainable because they cannot discipline themselves enough to provide the necessary information before the required deadline dates. If you are one of those people who almost prides yourself on procrastination, wise up. This is a way for you to get some financial help. Meet the deadlines.

The Battle for the Buck

Most people feel they never really have enough money, and during college, when so many demands are made on your limited financial resources, it would help to be a bit more careful with your spending habits. Check into all contracts you sign and be sure you understand the terms. Also, it might help to refer back to the previous chapter, on commuter colleges. Whether you are a commuter to a local school or are on a college or university main campus, the information at the end of that chapter will help.

Remember reading about the need for a word processor? The initial outlay for a machine, if you buy a new one, can be great. You may investigate purchasing a used one or renting. There are businesses around all colleges where there are rentals, sometimes with the option to buy at the end of the rental term, and this might be a more feasible way out of that expense.

Whether you own or rent a word processor, the money spent here is really a saving. Owning and using your own machine is much cheaper than paying to have your papers typed. It will also free you to do work when you want to and give you the opportunity to make revisions right up to the time you hand in the paper. Some students actually turn their word processing equipment into a money maker on campus. Those who can type fairly well can do work for others, charging appropriate fees for every page and paper processed.

Part-Time Jobs
Many students in commuter colleges spend almost as many hours working as they spend in the classroom. Whether you are a commuting student or a resident, you may be interested in some kind of employment that can add to your income.

First look within your own school. There are many places to look for a job: in dorms, with food services, in the campus bookstore, at the library, or even on a school publication. However, before you look for that job, it might be good to ask yourself a few questions. Can you handle the hours a particular job might require? Will you still have enough time for study, social life, and your own general sense of sanity? For instance, if your classes are very demanding and are a challenge to you, it may be better to borrow money or apply for financial assistance rather than give up necessary study time for a part-time job.

Here again, some honest discussion at home should give you a realistic picture of your family's financial situation. You should have been aware of the Financial Aid Form your parents filled out when you were a senior in high school. Now you should investigate family finances again. Has anything changed? You may never have been allowed to know how much your father or mother makes a year, and your parents may have kept you purposely in the dark about family finances. You're old enough for a lot of things now, and you owe it both to your parents and to yourself to be realistically aware of your family's financial situation. The more you understand about your folks' position and the more they understand yours, the easier it will be to clear the air and face finances and the need for study time honestly.

Also, if there is divorce in the family, remember that you may have the right to financial assistance during your college years, depending on the terms of your parents' divorce decree. Do some investigation, and if you need to get legal assistance to secure the money due you, don't be afraid to take that step. Most counties and states have agencies that make sure absent parents pay their share of costs for their children, and these can include college costs.

College-Style Cost Control It is possible to control a lot of the incidental costs of daily college life. How much you need "munchies," for instance, and how often you eat out definitely can affect your budget, to say nothing of some habits you may have developed along the lines of partying or drinking.

Many college students spend a lot of money for food—most of it junk food. While you may feel that a certain amount of this is necessary to your life-style, it would be wise to consider using cafeteria services more and curtailing your need for extra food. Hinting for a care package from home once in a while might help, too! Eating out may provide a change of scenery, but those meals away from campus tend to add up very quickly. Look at your eating habits and your life-style, and decide where some changes may be possible.

There are a few students on each campus who, when money gets tight, decide to skip meals in order to save money for other things. While you may feel this is all right, your health is too important to risk. Missing a meal once in a while won't hurt, but getting into the habit of doing this can cause serious trouble later on. If you are that desperate for money, see your counselor or check the job board.

The amount of money you spend on supplies can also be a big chunk of your budget, if you let it. Your college emblem on a notebook or folder may look impressive, but you can get school supplies much cheaper in an ordinary store. College bookstores have never been considered bargain basements! When you feel you need supplies, in fact, it may be worth a trip away from campus to do your shopping. Most stores near colleges tend to raise their prices because they know they have a captive market. Therefore, the farther away from school you can get to make your purchases, the more money you'll probably save. Look for big discount stores. The best thing you can do is lay in your supplies at home before you take off for college. That's where you'll save the most money.

You may never have worked with a budget in your life. There are many people who feel it's beneath their dignity or who decide they simply don't need it or don't have the discipline to follow one if they did make it. Keeping track of your expenses for a month or two, however, may show you some interesting patterns in your spending habits. Once you can see where money is going, you might be able to make a more realistic approach toward how and where you spend it.

Be careful with credit cards and cash. If you tend to carry a large amount of money with you, or have a copy of your folks' credit card, you can get into the habit of spending money too freely. Any funds that leave your wallet or a checkbook, even if they're on "plastic," are still money gone. Remember that, and if you need some help understanding your spending habits better, just jot down where you've spent money in the last month. Then decide if it was all really worth it.

Automatic teller machines (ATMs) can be a godsend when you really need your money but the bank is closed. However, they easily can be abused if you're not careful. Resist the temptation to nab cash for spur-of-the-moment purchases. And also keep your receipts and record them in your checkbook.

A further note on credit cards. The number of personal bankruptcies grows every year. This is often due to the great amount of purchases people put on their charge cards. If you can get in the habit of buying only what you can pay for, you'll be far ahead of the game in the finances of adult life.

If you are fortunate enough to have extra money on hand from time to time, you may also be a prime target for that friendly, glad-handing individual—the campus borrower. If you flash money around a lot, it won't take long for others to start thinking of you as a convenient lending institution and begin putting in their requests for a few dollars now and then. Be careful about lending money. Be sure you know exactly when you can expect it back. Lending money is rarely a good idea. It breaks up more friendships and causes more misunderstanding than almost anything else. And if you are one of those individuals who feels lending money adds to your popularity, you're looking in the wrong places for friendship.

Be careful, too, about where you do your banking. Most college students use the same bank, usually located close to campus. If you don't want to wait in long lines before vacations, you may consider going a little farther away from your living quarters, where you know you'll get quicker service. You should also have your savings at home in a local bank. Working from a budget, you won't be tempted to dip into that savings during the school year. Let that interest grow, and save your money there for another semester.

Many banks also have free checking. If there's one in your general area, consider using it rather than paying for each check. It may also be worth your time to spend a few minutes with one of the officers of your bank, just to find out what services are available to college students. Modern banking has reached a point where it can offer a lot of assistance in certain areas. However, if you don't take the time to learn what those services are, you'll never know what you may be missing, and what you could be saving.

Expect the Unexpected

While you're in college, it is important that you learn to be financially prepared for the unexpected. Cars have a way of breaking down, just as clothes have a way of wearing out. Extra cash on hand is almost as important to making it through school as is having a place to sleep or making sure you eat enough.

If summer jobs provide extra money for you, you could consider leaving most of that cash in a bank or with your parents. When many young people see that large sum of money at the end of a summer, they go back to campus thinking they'll be able to handle most financial demands.

The problem with knowing you have money available is that you feel too free to spend it. If you can keep most of it deposited away from you, and remember the long period of time through which that money must last, it will be easier to resist an expensive outfit or a new CD player once you are in a store somewhere near school. All those stores around your school are there for a reason. They all stay in business because they know many college students shop impulsively and often want to be seen where others shop. Give this attempt at popularity a back seat and save some money. Things are much cheaper away from campus. Wait until you get there to buy.

Be careful, too, about how much you spend on others. It's all right to feel the need to give a present now and then as a token of friendship or appreciation. But if you feel you must constantly give to people in order to keep them as friends, you may be doing them a disservice and hampering your own possibilities of making good friends on the merits of your own personality, interests, and individuality.

Living within Your Means

Only you know your exact financial situation and the circumstances of your family. You'll find people on any campus who have less money than you and students who have more. What you should begin to realize is that, because college is such a great melting pot, many people of different economic backgrounds can live and share together without letting money get in the way. Whether you have a lot of money or a little, learn to deal with others on a realistic and human level. The less money is involved with the most important things in your life, the better off you'll be.

People in many other countries think of the United States as a place where materialism overrides basic human qualities. If you find yourself needing more and more things, take a little break, sit back, and begin to think of the many facets of life that can make you feel rich without ever spending a dime. Money is always a tool, and it is obviously good to have. Just make sure it isn't the be-all and end-all of your life. Your happiness can never be measured by the amount of money you have. Remember that, and learn to use money as a servant to you, not the other way around.

Self-Check

1. How many sacrifices are your parents making so you can attend college? Be specific.

   _____

2. How would you describe your family's financial status?

   _____

   How much are you willing to help pay for your college expenses, and what are you doing about it?

   _____

3. What were your four most foolish purchases in the last few months?

   _____

   _____

   _____

   _____

4. How can you avoid making those same mistakes again? Is it the people you shop with? Is it your own impetuosity? Explain.

   _____

   _____

5. Do you have a budget? _____ What would it take to make you keep one for even one semester?

   _____

6. What would you find in your expenses if you recorded money spent over a two-month period? Where would be the first place to save?

   _____

   _____

7. Do you think others consider you materialistic? _____

   Explain. _____

8. Is the career you are planning one you really want, or are you choosing it simply because of the money you think you can make?

   _____

   _____

Facing the Folks

15

Meanwhile, Back at Home ...

As the rest of your life is moving on, one of the most important changes for you to comprehend is the difference in the relationship between you, your parents, and your brothers and sisters. In today's world there may be stepparents and stepbrothers and stepsisters due to divorce and remarriage. Your family may be quite an extended one, with a parent away from the home or deceased.

For most of your life you may have thought of your parents as authority figures, people who could dictate almost every move you made. They had real control over you, and though you have loved them, you may also have resented their power over you. You may feel they still don't understand you, and that feeling isn't going to help your maturing process through these college years.

Once you have made that leap from high school to college, things change—sometimes very suddenly and sometimes very dramatically. Your relationship with your folks cannot continue the way it was. You are a young adult now with greater desires for freedom and the need to feel independent and responsible for your own life. You know it, and you hope your parents know it, too.

No matter what your situation at home was during high school, once you enter college it's time to reassess your family relationships. True, your parents may not want to realize you're as old as you are. They may be fearful and think you may not be able to handle the freedom and responsibility you suddenly have, especially if you are away from home. As a result, there may be a lot of tension and a certain amount of mistrust once you've packed those bags and headed off to school. Even if you are still at home and commuting to school, your folks also know you are meeting different kinds of people, and their frustration about not knowing a lot of your new friends may cause tension.

Your parents realize, and probably you do, too, that once you are in college you will never be part of your family and your home in quite the same way again. If you are on a distant campus, there will be visits, but that's just what they'll be—visits. Your bedroom may still be there, but other members of the family already may be considering it for various other uses. Home will soon no longer be the safe haven you reach every night. Your world has gotten much larger now. As a result, your life within the home and the family has turned a very big corner.

The thought of not really belonging at home any more may make you sad, and in a way it should, because a precious part of your life has slipped away. Some students on campus cannot make the adjustment to living away from home, probably because they're not ready to be off on their own. They sometimes quit school for no other reason than their need to be close to family and home. They still feel the need to remain part of that safe nest called "my house." Others with aging parents also feel the distance too painful and return to a local school in order to help out on the home front.

Your Parents' Adjustments

Because your parents themselves are going through a great adjustment now that you are in college, it may be up to you to help your relationship with them move into a more mature and healthy area. This may even require a certain amount of forgiveness on your part. No one ever taught your parents how to handle their job in the future. No one ever gave them a degree in the lively art of parenting. They have gone fairly much on their own instincts and understanding of you, and as a result, they may have made some mistakes while you were young or growing through your teen years.

If you are the oldest, your parents may feel your loss at home as a loss of part of their own youth. If you are the youngest, watching you move on to college can make your parents feel the last contact with raising children is over. Whatever feelings your leaving brings, both you and your parents will have to deal with them. While some parents enjoy the fact they can now have their home and their lives more to themselves, there are others who see high school graduation as a pivotal point in their own lives. Try to understand this.

You may have felt your parents were overprotective. You may have felt they didn't care enough. They may have trusted you and let you grow, or they may have kept you purposely sheltered as much as possible, fearing your friends and all the trouble that might come to you.

As you look back over your relationship with your parents during high school, it would be good to consider it as a thing of the past. There is no way it can continue now in the same way; you have come too far, and you have too many miles still to travel.

This is a time to develop a new relationship with each of your parents, as well as with your brothers and sisters. Part of adulthood is being able to forget the past and to let relationships flow into new dimensions that will be normal and best for all concerned. It probably will be up to you to help your folks understand how you have grown, and how you are changing. It's hard on them, you know, to realize that you are slipping away from their influence. Others are talking to you now. You're getting advice and direction from different people, and your parents may feel left out. They worry about you. Do these new people really know you as well as they do? Do they truly understand all your needs? Are they sufficiently aware of your psychological makeup and what is necessary to your feeling of personal success? Or are they using you? Are they potentially harmful to you? These are all concerns parents have. You'll have them, too, when your own children are in the same place of life as you are now.

If you think this is a hard time for you, turn away from the mirror and look at the people with whom you have lived for most of your life. It's an equally hard time for them, too!

Building Mutual Respect

If there are any bad feelings from your high school days concerning your family, your first step should be to attempt to put those isolated incidents into the past and resolve to move on. The relationship between parents and their children changes when those children become adults. A mutual respect should grow. Also, an appreciation for each other's individuality and the demands of each person's life should develop.

For example, you should begin to see the different pressures your parents face in their own lives. You may realize now, more than ever, how much finances affect their lifestyle and the tensions they have. For example, maybe you'll begin to realize that your father isn't terribly happy in his job any more because he feels no challenge and gets no real satisfaction from the work he does. He may have lost his job and must content himself with doing something else now, which was not his first choice of employment. Yet he stays at it, partly because he may need its security, or he may need to keep supplying you with money during these college years.

Your growing relationship with the folks should also bring about a new sensitivity toward the changes in your parents' personality and ambitions. Your mother and father, whether they are together or apart, are now in middle age. They may have settled in, and they may not be happy about it. You, with your life stretching ahead with almost limitless possibilities open to you, have the luxury of making mistakes and still having enough time to find yourself and your place in the world.

Your folks, on the other hand, may feel their best years are behind them: seeing you leave home, they may begin to feel an emptiness or a certain staleness in their lives. As you move toward maturity and adulthood, part of your great contribution to your parents and your entire family will be an understanding of those subtle changes in attitude. Continue to love those who have been so special all your life. If you expect your parents to ride with you through all the changes up ahead, a little understanding and sensitivity on your part now will go a long way.

Reversing the Charges

Communication is the key for almost every situation in life, and as you deal with your folks from your position as a college student, it becomes even more critical. They still care, but they may not know how to let you know of their continued interest. They don't want to seem nosy or show a lack of faith in your ability to handle the changes you are facing. They honestly want you to feel success in your new independence. Believe that!

Now that you are away from home, or commute to school from there, your parents only know what you choose to tell them. Realistically, they will understand that certain areas of your life may be kept from them. This is especially true if they know you weren't totally honest with them during your high school years. For example, if you drank or smoked while you were in high school and never told your parents, they have probably guessed that it wasn't just all the smell of people smoking around you that came home on your clothes, but they may have chosen to let you make your own choices.

Your parents may have been wary of your friends while you were in high school, and now that they have less opportunity to meet the people with whom you spend most of your time, they may be even more concerned that you are under some strong negative influences or that you are being led in directions they feel aren't right for you. Are you involved with someone they don't know? Are you caught up in the wrong crowd, doing the wrong things?

What you choose to tell your parents is, of course, up to you. The most important thing is that you do stay in honest communication. They need to be reassured that you are surviving, that you are at least coping with everyday life at school, and that you are experiencing a certain amount of happiness.

How does this happen? Keep in touch. Write. Call. Whatever means you choose, try not to become so busy that you don't have time to drop them a line or pick up a phone and make a call home. More than ever, your college years are a vital time for communication between you and the rest of your family, and if you still have them, this includes grandparents. Often a short note, call, or visit from you is the highlight of their day or week.

The habits of staying in touch that you develop now, in your first real experience away from home, will set the tone for how much communication there will be in later years, when the miles between you may be much greater, but when the love and interest can be no less real. Share with your folks. They really want to know what you're thinking and what is important to you now. Even though there may have been unhappy times before, your parents are excited about your future, and they are proud of the very fact you are attending college. Tell them at least enough to let them know they are still very much on your mind and still very much in your heart.

Grow with Them, Not Away from Them

Your adult life is right around the corner, and as you approach it, don't feel you have to approach it alone. No matter what has happened in the past, your family will remain your first and last defense against pressures and problems. True, you are not under your parents' control so much any more. You are well on your way to independent adulthood.

That independence, however, in no way includes the feeling that your family is now a thing of the past, that you don't need them any more, and that you can go on without them. Too many good things have happened between you and different family members. Too many precious moments and happy times are tucked away somewhere in your memory and, if you intend to live a complete adult life, your continuing relationship with all members of your family, at whatever age they are or where they may be, will be essential.

Forgive, if you have to forgive. Understand what needs to be understood. Put yourself in your parents' position as adults, now that you are so close to adulthood yourself. Don't look upon your leaving home as an escape from tyranny or a chance to finally be yourself. You are just moving on into the world of adulthood, and that move can happen very easily and naturally with your family remaining a positive and constant part of your life.

There will come a time up ahead, you know, when your parents will start relying on you, just as you have relied on them in the past. They may turn to you for advice and for help, just as, presumably, you have turned to them. The relationship between parents and adult children is one of mutual giving and taking, and as the years move on, it is the children who start doing most of the giving.

Remember that your parents are not the enemy; they never have been. They are just people who have tried as best they could to give you what they honestly felt you needed at different stages of your life.

Your brothers and sisters, no matter what age, may have been going through problems of their own. They, too, are moving on, and if you can move with them and let them know where you are and where you feel you are going, your relationships with them can be precious.

You want others to know what you have become and what you are becoming. Give your family members the same opportunity to know that you, too, are aware of their pain, their joys, and their successes.

Self-Check

1. On a scale of 1–10, with 10 being highest, how would you rate your honesty and openness with your parents?

   _____

   _____

2. What areas of your life are unknown to your parents, and why?

   _____

   _____

3. How often do you try to communicate with your parents?

   _____

   Is this all right with you? _____

   If not, what is keeping you from more communication?

   _____

4. Do you set times to contact your parents? _____

   Would this help or not help you remember to stay in touch with them?

   _____

5. To what extent do you use your schoolwork or your busy schedule as excuses for not writing or calling home?

   _____

6. How important do you feel your family is in your life now?

   _____

7. How aware are you of the pressures and problems your parents are experiencing now?

   _____

8. Write a short essay describing your past relationship with your family and what is is like now. Mention the family member who causes you the most concern and what you hope for that person and your future relation-ship with him or her.

_____

_____

_____

_____

_____

_____

_____

Housing—Haven or Hassle?

Roomies, Rumors, and Reality

Once you leave home, one of the biggest adjustments you must make to college life is living on your own or with someone who doesn't know you that well. You start off as strangers who don't know any of the circumstances of each others' lives before the time you both stand in the room you are suddenly sharing. You're each an unknown quantity, but you must accept one another, for better or worse!

Many college students find some of their greatest pressures not from class or home, but from sharing a room with someone who comes from another part of the state or country and who may have very different values and a different life-style from their own.

One of the greatest secrets for succeeding in college, and in life, is adaptability. Leaving home, where everything was set and comfortable, where everyone knew you and knew what they could expect from you, is hard enough. Coming into a new situation where different demands are being made on you can be hard, but having to go "home" to a room where there may be even more problems and more intense pressures can almost push you to the breaking point. You need to feel comfortable and relaxed at certain times of the day, and because of this, housing is one of the most important aspects of success in your college career if you are away at campus.

Little Things Mean a Lot

No matter where you live—in a dorm, fraternity or sorority house, or an apartment off campus—it is important that the person or persons with whom you live are compatible with you. For example, smokers and nonsmokers often clash. Try to find someone whose choice in this regard matches yours. Likewise, a teetotaler and a party animal could encounter trouble living together.

Even little things such as taste in music, sleeping habits, and amount of study time needed should have some degree of compatibility in those four walls that make up your room. Realize, though, that there will be things about you that irritate your roommate, just as he or she may have habits or attitudes that get under your skin.

Most housing administrators try to leave a certain amount of flexibility as far as rooming assignments go. Even though it is often a lot of work to reassign rooms, these people have realized the importance of where you live and with whom you live. Thus, if you feel a change is necessary to your continued sanity and success, they'll often agree to make the arrangements for a change in housing.

You can save yourself a lot of trouble, however, by doing a little homework before you decide to room with a certain person, or, if you are an older student, decide where you'll live. Many schools require freshmen and sophomores to live on campus and in dorms. Incoming freshmen, new to the area and often feeling the pain of being away from home for the first prolonged time, are tempted to room with old friends from high school. They may feel a certain amount of security doing this; it's easier than risking the possibility of not getting along with a total stranger. However, this can backfire when the friendship buckles under the added strain of living together.

When choosing roommates, it is best not to hang on so tightly to security that you don't leave room for new people and new experiences. If you have good friends from high school who are on campus with you, you will continue to socialize with them. Remember that one of the great assets of attending school away from home is the fact you are free to develop yourself in different situations and learn how to cope with new people.

Where, Oh Where?

If dormitory living is required or is your choice for housing, you should be familiar enough with your school to choose a dorm where you'll feel most comfortable. Many colleges have some dorms that carry stricter rules for social hours, study time, and visitor access. If you feel your class schedule or your life-style suggest you need a little more peace in order to do your best work, don't bend to the pressure of friends who do all they can to get housing in a "party dorm."

Some dorms, just as some fraternity or sorority houses, may get labeled, and you'll need to set the record straight if you find yourself and your living quarters being stereotyped or judged. Some students feel that frat or sorority houses are snobbish and restrictive; others feel this isn't the case at all. What remains most important is that you feel comfortable wherever you live. Forget peer pressure and image, and choose to live where you feel things will be most comfortable for you given your life-style.

Should You Pledge?

On some campuses, especially in smaller schools, fraternities and sororities are socially important. You'll have to look at your own school and the Greek organizations available before deciding if you want to pledge one. Some colleges and universities may downplay their importance, while on some campuses their existence in the mainstream of student life is a necessity that is almost taken for granted. Just remember, there are all kinds of people on any college campus. There is security in the Greek organizations, and another form of identity which can help you feel you belong. However, you will need to spend more money to be part of the Greek system because dues and other fees are charged.

If you feel it's right for you, go ahead and think about trying to join. Pledging, Rush Week, and your early days in the house may be rough, and you run the risk of not being accepted. If belonging to one of these groups is important to you, go for it!

On the other hand, if you feel you must pledge a Greek organization just to fit in and be accepted socially, you haven't looked around your campus enough. There are many individuals and smaller special interest groups that give a lot to each other. You may save money and a certain amount of social pressure by lining up with them rather than with a fraternity or sorority.

As you move along toward adulthood, you should be more aware of how your life-style differs from others, what you need, and where you feel most at home. Whether that place is a dorm, a Greek house, or an apartment off campus, that's where you should be. Just don't bow to pressures when it comes to housing. It is a very important part of your college career. You are growing a lot during these years, and the changes in you should be reflected in your ever-refining choice of housing. It's one place where others will begin to see your ability to handle important aspects of your life.

Living Off Campus

When your college permits it, you may have the option to move off campus to an apartment or house. Many college towns cater to student boarders, and you should have little trouble finding a place to stay if you start looking early enough. If you feel you would prefer this type of living, it would be wise to check out the people you'll be sharing it with very carefully. Because you are away from campus, you'll also be away from most campus rules, and you'll be more independent than you've ever been before. Big question here—can you handle it?

Are the people who will share that apartment or house with you compatible in most areas? Will you be able to work out a set of satisfactory "house rules" where social life, study time, and hours for relaxing can be agreed upon by all? Will you be able to handle money problems that arise? Food bills may seem like a trivial matter, but you could find yourself splitting a food bill three ways and feeling you're not getting your share of what is bought. A situation like this can very quickly cause a lot of frustration and possible misunderstanding. With your roommates' friends dropping over and possibly eating too much of what you bought, it doesn't take long for a tense situation to develop. Clear the air of these concerns before you agree to share living expenses and living space with others.

Transportation back to campus also should be worked out. Cars, work schedules, and class hours may become extremely important. Make sure you have these details covered before you locate out in the boondocks and away from the mainstream of college life.

Living off campus can be demanding as well as enjoyable. You are cut off there from the rest of the world in a most unique way. There are no parents, no authority figures around. It is simply you and your friends against the universe! Life off campus can be beneficial and a real asset to your development as a person. In a way, you could consider off-campus housing as your first apartment. This style of living, however, can also be the cause of one of your greatest migraines. Take an honest look at yourself and a very realistic look at your prospective roommates. Weigh the circumstances, and then make your decision as realistically as possible.

Odd Coupling

No matter where you are in your college experience, your roommate has the ability to make your life truly comfortable or truly miserable.

If your roommate is incorrigible, or you find yourself totally at odds with her or him most of the time, you can always request a change. It is possible, however, to set up certain rules that can make life in your room a lot more agreeable for both of you. Expenses, for example, are one area you should discuss and agree upon. Get a firm commitment from your roommate regarding the cost of the phone, refrigerator, or anything else you both feel the room needs. Do you want extra bookcases, and maybe an extra chair or two? Who will pay for these things, and when you break up housekeeping, who is going to get that furniture?

Some roommates even draw an invisible line across a room in hope of maintaining a few square yards of living space that at least give the semblance of privacy. One of the most basic human needs we all have is a sense of turf, a sense of a place of our own. When you were little, you may have enjoyed playing in a new appliance carton. You did that because you liked being in your own space. That part of you hasn't changed. It merely has become more sophisticated. If you feel drawing a line in your room is necessary, you can try it, but it usually doesn't work. Noise has a way of going through invisible lines, just as attitudes drift freely through space.

If you feel you can realistically set aside certain parts of your room where some studying can be done or where you can relax, by all means work it out with your roommate. A better solution to living in one room with someone, however, is an agreement on priorities for time, space, and furnishings. This again is one instance where little things mean a lot. One solution is to have an alternative site for serious study, thus leaving the room as a place where a certain amount of normal living can take place.

If you are tidy but your roommate tends to be somewhat on the messy side, you may find yourself living an "odd couple" situation in which you get increasingly frustrated as you try to keep your room from looking like a tornado went through. If your roommate wants to party and socialize quite often and some of your classes force you into extra study time, who leaves the room, you or your roommate?

When thinking about problems such as these, solutions seem simple. Since living together is such a consuming psychological situation, however, it would be best to sit down with your roommate and discuss certain situations or problems that easily can arise. Running through a set of hypothetical situations and assessing both your reactions to these situations will give you some good insights into how someone will react before you actually move in and start to live through a year of hectic college life.

Another subtle situation that can arise between roommates is the possibility of competition. Is your roomie the type who never studies, yet manages to pull down consistently better grades than you? Is he or she more attractive or more popular? Is your roommate the type who can eat anyone under the table and never gain an ounce, while you struggle to take off pounds? Competition is very common. It's almost a basic human tendency to compare oneself with others from time to time. The only problem with this is that you usually feel it is you who comes out on the short end of all those comparisons!

Once you can zero in on some acceptable rules for living with your roommate or roommates, do yourself one more favor and learn to accept those people, period! True, he, she, or they may be smarter than you, or may have certain qualities you envy. Accept your roommate for what he or she is, and be positive enough about yourself to allow that person's acceptance of you, too, as a unique individual with your own gifts, dreams, and special talents to offer.

On the Fringes Floormates? Doesn't sound like a terrific description for anyone. However, if you have lived for more than a few weeks on campus, you know very well how important that fringe of people who share your dorm floor with you really is.

In most dorms there are students who work as part-time

counselors, handling situations on each floor of a dorm. This is often a thankless job since they also are asked to help enforce rules. Get to know the people in charge of your floor as more than occasional faces behind the desk. If you are on speaking terms with them, you won't be coming in from left field to argue with the umpire when you want to lodge a complaint or make a suggestion or request.

If you have chosen your dorm wisely, you should be able to find a certain amount of compatibility with most people on your floor. Also, if you decide someone is abusing privileges or is making life difficult for you and for others, you should feel free enough to approach that person first or to lodge a legitimate complaint with your floor supervisor or counselor.

Remember when we discussed leadership? If you are a quiet type who always follows, you may mutter under your breath and complain to your roommate about situations that aggravate you. What you should do is show some initiative and try to do something about problems you feel are interfering with the calm and sane state of your dorm. If things are getting to you, don't be afraid to speak up once in a while and let others know what is bothering you.

Where you live and how you live can be controlled to a large extent by you. If you let others know when you feel things could be better, and offer some solid advice toward making them better, you'll find others coming to you often in friendship and in that great general feeling of camaraderie that can develop on campus.

Communicate. Be as positive as you can, and offer realistic and fair suggestions without being belligerent or domineering. The people who share your living quarters—in your room, on your floor, or in your off-campus apartment—can become lifelong friends. They can contribute much to your happiness at school. Give them that chance to be themselves. Accept those who really know you and still like you, and do your best to be a positive, open, and friendly person.

The people with whom you live can be some of the most frustrating individuals in your life. They can also be some of the best. Give them a chance, and give yourself a chance for those good friendships, too!

Self-Check   1. How honest do you feel you usually are with people?

2. On a scale of 1–10, with 10 being the highest, how would you rate your ability to get along with people?

   _____

3. What is your usual way to handle difficulties with people, and how could it be improved?

   _____

4. What would you suggest are key topics you should discuss with any possible roommate before you begin sharing space.

   _____

   _____

5. How sensitive are you to others' needs? _____

6. Could you be accused of selling yourself out for popularity or avoiding personal discussions that could make for better understanding? Explain.

   _____

   _____

7. What specific things could be done now to ease any tensions that exist in your living situation? Be specific, and detail your part in this effort.

   _____

   _____

   _____

8. Would you describe yourself as easy or difficult to live with? Explain your answer.

   _____

   _____

   _____

Sex, Drugs, and Rock 'n' Roll

17

The Choice Is Yours

Many a student has heard about the "wild" side of college life away from home. With no Mom and Dad looking over your shoulder, you're free to make your own choices about personal matters. The folks won't be waiting up for you, ready to tell you off for staying out too late or grilling you like the Spanish Inquisition about where you were and with whom. No one will be keeping tabs on what you drink or eat—no one but you, that is. For some students, college is an acid test of their personal values. They must decide what they really believe as opposed to how they acted because parents or friends expected it.

This chapter will get into some very tough topics and challenges for you, but here it's time to take a good look at your attitudes toward life, yourself, and your future. How you view your past and present are important, too, because they give a hint on how you will perform in the years ahead.

Whatever your past has been—however many corners you have been around—it is now time to consider what you are and what you are becoming. The attitude you take to any social gathering is the attitude that will lay the foundation for your future.

Watch Your Feet and Head

Remember back in high school when people talked about peer pressure? Many people told you it had an effect on your life, and until you make that giant leap into true adulthood, it will continue to affect you. True independence is the mature realization that there is no need to go along with others to be accepted. You may have reached that point; you may have not.

You may decide to always be one of those who follows the crowd and most often goes along with everyone else rather than risk ridicule or disapproval. Or, you may choose to make the break from peer pressure and pull away from the dictates of the majority. How much you are willing to give up your own principles for popularity and social acceptance will determine how much you are willing to follow your own head.

And here the questions become—how good is your head, and how good are your feet? Can you use your head wisely? Are you able to stand on your own two feet?

Everyone needs acceptance; that's a fact of life. How much you need it, though, depends on how secure you are within yourself. There are adults who never quite overcome the pressure to be accepted by the crowd. They look to neighbors, friends from work, and everyone else for constant approval. They even gear their entertainment and leisure activities into avenues they think are acceptable.

Peer pressure sometimes translates into the materialistic area, such as with clothes, car, house, and job, but it can also be much more subtle. You may be the type of person who needs others' approval of your life-style, your values, and how you choose to live, even to the point of having the "right" number of children or acting the "right" way with your spouse. True, you need acceptance just as does anyone else. The real answer, however, lies in learning how to accept yourself!

College can be a big help in winning the battle against peer pressure. Because you are on your own, it can help you develop the ability to be secure within yourself and realize your power over your own life. Many high school students, and you may have been one of them, look forward to the day they'll get out from their parents' authority. In too many cases, though, the new-found freedom of college is lost to any strong individual who can take over as an undue influence in their lives. If you feel that someone else is holding too much sway in your life, first of all make your feet go very quickly in any direction away from that person. Then stop and stand on them—on your own!

Sexual Attitudes   One of the biggest challenges to any young person is the development of healthy sexuality, and your generation must forge its own way.

Your grandparents probably grew up in the "dark ages" when sex was a taboo topic and the lack of reliable birth control methods made unwanted pregnancy the biggest fear of heterosexual couples, even married ones. Abortion was illegal. Venereal diseases could be fatal.

If your parents came of age during the 1960s, they faced a sexual environment of unparalleled freedom. The topic of sex could be discussed more openly. The pill had come onto the market as an effective method of birth control, and by 1973 abortion was legal. Suddenly heterosexual couples did not have to fear unwanted pregnancy. Medical breakthroughs made death from venereal disease a thing of the past. Some homosexuals took advantage of the more permissive climate to "come out of the closet." Sex without marriage bore less of a stigma, and some people experimented with numerous partners.

Then along came AIDS. It slammed shut the window of opportunity that had been opened a generation earlier. Moral implications aside, casual sexual involvement now can cost you your life. AIDS is spread primarily through sexual contact, so if you have sex with a person who is infected with the AIDS-producing HIV virus, you could contract the virus and end up with AIDS. To date, AIDS has no cure. If you contract it, you will likely die within 5–10 years.

Even with all the condom ads and discussion you hear, you must be aware that "safe sex" won't always protect you. While condoms do help prevent the transmission of the HIV virus and prevent pregnancy, they are not 100 percent effective. Only abstinence is. This does not mean you must remain celibate all your life, but you'd better be prepared to stake your life on your choice of partner.

Time to Learn

The fact remains that the social scene, especially dating, has become a tangled web of sexual involvement for many. Once a couple in high school starts dating on a regular basis, some people may assume they have gotten into an arena that involves sexual activity. This attitude no only may weaken the respect an individual might have for himself or herself; it also may set a tone of expected permissiveness.

As a result of this early experience, some college students have decided it is in their best interest not to date at all. Young women who are tired of fighting off their dates' demands, and young men who would rather not have to go through the pressure for sexual performance stay away from the dating scene. As you face society in which sex is taken for granted much too often, the only way you can survive is by understanding yourself and your perspective on dating, giving and taking, and—most importantly—your own attitude toward love.

It's Only Natural!

Everyone needs love. No one would argue with that. One of the most normal and natural feelings you have is your desire to love and be loved. No one wants to go through life feeling uncared for and sensing that all the love inside him or her is wasted and lost. If love is an intrinsic part of the human spirit, it is also an intrinsic part of human nature to share love with others.

As great as people's need for love is, so is the lack of adequate education on what real love is all about. This is one reason for the problems so many people seem to have. There are songs and poems about love. Movies and booksellers do brisk business telling and retelling love stories. However, while everyone seems to make quite a big stir about this greatest of all human feelings, few try to understand it.

Perhaps the biggest misconception about love is that it exists usually and most powerfully only in the physical state. Of course, physical reactions are a lot easier to comprehend than feelings. The advertising as well as entertainment industries have made sure we are constantly bombarded with the physical aspects of love. It isn't always as easy to look beyond the body and physical qualities. It takes more sensitivity and awareness.

Some background on the ancient Greeks might give a better understanding of the essence of love. Those Greeks, who were noted for their wisdom, reasoned that because love is so complex, there are really three different stages to it. The least important of these stages, *Eros,* they decided, is physical or sensual love. Even animals have this love. It is natural to all procreating species.

The second type of love they called *Philos,* the word from which we get words such as *philosophy* (love of wisdom) and *philharmonic* (love of music). This type of love is more a love of the mind, in which two people understand each other and share much more than what two bodies can possibly offer. This is a love most common between friends and relatives but also required for anyone who contemplates marriage. The Greeks knew that physical attraction does not always last, so they suggested that before two people marry, they must develop a love of the mind, whereby they are capable of sharing on a higher level.

The third kind of love, *Agapos,* not reached by most, is a love of the spirit. In this love there is a sharing of ideas as well as of deep human feelings. In this love the sensitivities are right, and both people are completely honest with each other. They share each other's soul. This kind of love, according to the Greeks, is a love in which two spirits meet and share, each respecting the other's individuality, but each understanding the other to such an extent that a beautiful bond is created, a bond of intense caring. In a love of this kind, the other person almost becomes an alter ego—another self. While two people remain unique, a part of each also manages to blend into the other. This is a love between sensitive, aware people—people are who leaders in their own lives and who are strong enough to accept the leadership and uniqueness of another.

If you are normal, you feel this tremendous need to love, and that's good. Be sure, though, that you understand what kind of love you really need. Don't be satisfied with substitutes or forms of loving others see as acceptable or commonplace. There is nothing commonplace about real love!

What Do You Expect?

Today's society often gives any individual the idea that sexual involvement is automatically presumed. It may be time to sit back and try to understand what is expected of you from the people you care about. Most of all, it is essential to understand what you expect from yourself. How great is your respect for yourself, and how susceptible are you to demands from others? The simple truth is that you probably want to date people who are compatible with you and with whom you can have a good time without being pressured. One of the last things you need in your life right now is more pressure, from any source!

This is the great time when you are becoming an individual, remember? Your parents are out of the way, and no one can make decisions for you. It's all up to you. If yours is the age of individuality, then start becoming an individual by asserting your own ideas and attitudes toward your own body and the bodies of others.

Thinking about Marriage

With more young women preparing for careers today, some of the pressure on them to marry and immediately begin a family has lessened. The job market is open to both sexes on a more equal basis now, thus early marriage seems to be getting less common.

Because the young adult world after college offers so many exciting opportunities, new people, and the chance of travel, more young people who realize they will marry sooner or later, opt for later. They want to experience some of that excitement. They want a chance to succeed and experience professional fulfillment before settling down to family life. This is the age of the career woman and the liberated man. Because of this, marriage among young adults is on the decline. Sexual involvement, however, is not.

One problem with becoming overinvolved with someone you might be dating is that, after you have reached this point, you may feel you must make a decision. Some couples in this position decide to part ways. Others feel there is enough between them to keep on sharing, and they make the move into marriage.

Divorce courts seem to indicate that many people marry much too young, while they are still feeling the exhilaration of sexual involvement or that first flash of intense feeling and not thinking about the full implication of spending the rest of their lives together. The two lives may grow apart because the two people are moving in different directions. Then, too late, both partners realize they married before they knew what they really wanted and needed. The situation becomes even more complicated if the couple has had children.

Marriage at an early age presumes an average of 40 years of living together. This is almost mind-boggling when you think of it, and it's a good fact to remember before you make what may be the biggest move in your life.

Give yourself some time to establish perspective, and marry only after you feel you are aware of the consequences. Marriage isn't an escape from a bad home life, neither is it a solution to loneliness.

The Number One Drug

In a climate of "Just Say No to Drugs," the one that is most abused in the United States is legal—alcohol. The beer companies use handsome young men and nubile women to promote their products, and you can't help getting the idea that a fun party should include a bottomless keg.

If you choose to drink, you may need a bit of self-education. Somehow society expects you to know how to handle yourself when it comes to social drinking, but it never teaches you how to do it. You may have to learn the hard way before you understand your personal tolerance level. You should learn, too, what a full or empty stomach can do, and in the case of women, know how certain times of the month affect your toleration of alcohol.

Some college students slowly slip into alcoholism without even realizing it, using alcohol as a crutch for handling pressures. Take a look at the following list of questions and answer yes or no to each one.

_____ Do you find yourself getting drunk, even when you hadn't intended to?

_____ Do you drink to handle problems or relieve tension?

_____ Do you find yourself needing a drink more often, or wishing you had one?

_____ When you drink, do you drink quickly and gulp drinks down?

_____ Do you ever try to hide the fact that you're drinking?

_____ Do friends occasionally try to sober you up while you still try to explain that you are not drunk?

_____ Are changes occurring in your physical appearance or health habits?

_____ Do you find it harder to do well in courses that were once easy for you?

_____ Do you have insomnia, stomach trouble, headaches, or loss of appetite?

_____ Do you find your friends not as close as they once were, suddenly finding excuses not to go to a certain party with you or choosing to be somewhere else instead?

If you answer yes to any of these questions, this is a sign that you may be developing a dependence on alcohol, and with it a loss of your own independence as an individual. You can try to convince yourself that you still can handle the booze and that others are simply too straight-laced to understand your ability to drink. If you are honest, however, you'll begin to notice these subtle changes and realize that it may be time for you to decide to make some changes in your drinking habits. You may even want to quit for a while.

Furthermore, if you feel study belongs to the weekdays, but the weekends are yours to party and possibly drink too much, think again. There is no such thing as a weekend alcoholic. There are only alcoholics, period.

If you choose to drink, find the level of alcohol you can tolerate, and don't go past it.

Other Drugs

The fact that marijuana is illegal seems to carry little weight on most campuses. Music and entertainment glorify it and joke about it. You can buy T-shirts, charms, and belt buckles celebrating it. In fact, if you want to get your hands on some, it's easier to find in some dorms than a full bar of soap. Smoking marijuana is accepted as a reality in some people's lives and in their circle of friends. While school administrators frown about it and condemn it, most of them choose to do very little about it.

Because smoking pot is accepted as a reality by some, it's time for you to decide if it's going to be a reality for you. If so, go back to the alcohol checklist and substitute marijuana as the substance. Watch out for yes answers!

Cocaine and crack cocaine also have found ready markets on many campuses. The group who finds life too tedious or who may not be into the academic and social side of college life may choose to keep up a cocaine habit—until the habit chooses very quickly to keep them.

The danger of any artificial escape through alcohol or other drugs is that it begins to lull its user into believing it is the only alternative to constant pressure or an empty feeling of unfulfillment. No matter what that escape is, it leaves the person feeling unable to cope with problems and life's demands unless he or she is high or drunk. That's not only a cop-out, it's a disaster.

Finally, remember that you could be arrested for possession of illegal drugs, giving you a criminal record and possibly even landing you in jail. Is it worth that risk?

A Dose of Reality

If there were ever a time when the use of alcohol and drugs could be argued away, this may be the time, while you are going through all the demands of college. Many students feel that way and easily get sucked into the pattern of taking uppers to ensure the ability to study longer and meet deadlines, then downers to relax when some of the more stressful times are over.

Getting hooked on anything that does you no good happens slowly and insidiously, but it does happen. Taking that first upper and then "flying all night" as you prepare for an exam may seem an exhilarating experience at the time. It doesn't take long, however, before you'll need two pills to do what one used to, and then more and more. The human body isn't made to tolerate a lot of drugs.

When they realize what is happening to them in regard to drug or alcohol dependency, some people have the courage to stop while they still can. They feel their dependence growing and don't like what that need is doing to their bodies or their minds. In one last burst of personal energy, they decide to quit. For many others, such a decision seems always out of reach. By the time the need for it is crucial, it's often too late to find any energy left at all. If your friends or you are in that situation, don't make the mistake of thinking help will come once rock bottom is reached. Doctors and nurses in chemical dependency wards will give the sad answer there: "Rock bottom for some people is death, and there is no coming back from that."

College is not meant to be easy, just as it isn't meant to push you to the verge of a nervous breakdown. No one should need pills and artificial escapes to get through it. If you feel you have a weakness in this regard, there are places right on campus or nearby where you can get help. The greatest place you can begin, however, is by straightening out the priorities in your own head and deciding to take better care of yourself.

It is true that everyone needs some escapes from pressures and problems. It is also true that many people manage this need quite well without becoming dependent on alcohol or drugs. Your particular campus may have more than its share of alcoholics, potheads, pill poppers, and crack users. How you react to this scene and the temptation to misuse these substances is up to you. It's your head, it's your body, and it's your life!

Furthermore, if you make excuses for the addictions of others, you are an enabler. You make it easier for those people to continue in their addictions, and by not trying to help them out of their problems, you help them continue. You are not being a friend by doing that. You are, in a sense, part of your friends' problems.

Suicide Is Not Painless
You or one of your friends may reach such a low point one day that you seriously consider suicide. It remains the number one cause of death for young people. If you are ever tempted to kill yourself because of pressure or because you see no real future ahead of you, please stop and think. Try to remember that "this, too, shall pass." If you have so little fight in you and so little love for yourself, try looking around at the people who love you and whose lives would be much poorer if you weren't around. Think about them and what your death would do to them. Think about yourself, and then dare to dream just a little of how good things can be when you are on top of your own world. You don't need an escape to get there. You just need to believe in yourself.

And if you see any of your friends "setting things straight" suddenly, returning what was borrowed, giving things away, and acting suddenly too calm about their problems, get them help—fast. Those are signs of potential suicide.

Self-Check

1. What are the qualities of the ideal man or woman you would like to marry?

   _____

   _____

2. Do you feel your attitude toward sexual involvement is right for you?

   _____

   Does that attitude come from your own mind and feelings, or from what others expect of you? Explain.

   _____

   _____

3. What advice would you give a friend who is sexually involved and who wants to break off the relationship?

   _____

   _____

4. How has your attitude toward sex, AIDS, and your own physical needs changed over the past four years? Explain.

_____

_____

5. How do you feel about others who frequently use drugs or drink too much?

_____

Do others feel the same about you? Why or why not?

_____

6. How has your attitude toward drinking and drugs changed over the past five years?

_____

_____

7. How do you think you will treat liquor and drugs ten years from now?

_____

_____

They're Saying That . . . | 18

Facing and Beating the Raps

As we near the end of this book, it is only right that you face some of the more common accusations others make of your generation. It is also right that you get an opportunity to see if they apply to you, and then decide how you will move beyond college with the echo of them in your head.

The following are some of the most common comments made by employers and adults who deal with students or people recently graduated from college.

"They Have No Values"

This is an easy one. Most adults have seen enough news footage and read enough newspapers, as well as met enough college students who don't seem to have values. The number of young people who insist on pursuing their own pleasure at the risk of their jobs, friendships, and their own growth is numerous. They are the ones who get the press coverage, and they are the ones whose failures in the real world make people notice.

What you value may not be something you think of very much these days, but what you value and what you come to value will determine your attitude, not only during these years, but also in the immediate years after college. You are moving now farther away from youth and what some call its follies. With each year in college, people begin to look at you for signs of purposeful values. Do you look like you know where you're going? Do you know where you're going? Make sure your own priorities begin to move away from what is only "fun" toward what has substance. As your college years move along, prove to yourself that you are getting out of the party syndrome and into a more serious approach toward your career and working toward your first real job.

"They Don't Know the Meaning of Work"

An executive of a national insurance company recently confided, "I had to fire 50 people yesterday. It really bothered me. They were all under 28, and some of them had potential. But they had no loyalty to the company. All they cared about was big pay, top benefits, and how quickly the day would pass. They just didn't know how to work, and they had no intention of learning."

Sad words, sadder because that executive voices the concern of many employers who are beginning to look away from the youthful job market. A lot of young people who have preceded you into the work force have not set high standards for those who hire. Too many of them have also been people others have had to fire.

Some employers feel today's colleges are turning out graduates who do not know the meaning of an honest day's work. Of course that is not true for all. There are enough young people, however, who have not shown a solid work ethic as they embarked on chosen careers for which they have spent much money and time training.

You can assess your own work ethic in the way you approach the job you have now, which is being a student. You are getting no pay, and perhaps you may feel you give yourself pay by putting the books aside and seeing to your own pleasure. That may be fine for some. Yet by junior year in college, many of the people who keep this feeling are gone through failure or by just dropping out. Some large university campuses, especially those considered party schools, can chew up students and spit them out on a regular basis. When you do get the job that will begin the career you now seek, be sure you go to that first day of work with some honest realities tucked in your head. Your parents and everyone else has had to work for whatever they have achieved, and you also must prove to employers that you can be part of their team and be productive according to their priorities.

"All They Care About Is Themselves"

There are those who feel your generation doesn't care about anything. They feel that you think you know it all and that you do not want to learn more. They wonder if you can bring the planet back to any form of regrowth, and if you care about government, democracy, and all the dues people pay for being on the earth.

You do know many things, but do you form your own opinions about world events? Do you take time to analyze them and stay informed about them? An important step in growing up is learning to care about things outside yourself. Being a mature adult means giving up the self-absorption that is natural to children. As an adult, you are not only a responsible member of your own family and circle of friends, but you are also important to your community and to the world.

How do you prove that you care about more than yourself? Show concern. Show motivation, not only in your work, but in learning more about others and what concerns them. When an election nears, care enough to learn about the candidates and vote. Your age group has the lowest percentage of people who actually vote, with the result that most candidates never worry much about what is important to you. Register, then check out absentee ballots if you live on campus, but vote!

Follow through on things. Be responsible. Start feeling like someone who cares, and start acting like a person who has commitments, goals, and the willingness to see them accomplished.

Do Reality!

There are those who say your generation doesn't "do reality." They say you refuse to get involved with things that matter.

Your answer? Do reality! Care!

Care about the world in which you live. Care about your family members and friends. Care about your own ability to live responsibly and productively in the adult world. Don't be afraid to go out of your way to show concern for others. Try to overcome selfishness when you're tempted into it, and try to show you desire to know what the world is thinking and suffering. Get in the giving and caring mode.

Accept responsibility. Listen to others' criticism of your work, then consider their words and make a reasonable response. It is the child who always puts blame elsewhere. Show some motivation at school, at home, and in your life. Finish the projects you start and decide to make a valid contribution to the groups in which you hold membership. Show others you're not afraid of hard work and that you have the ability to see things through with honest effort. People will always find fault with the younger generation. Face their accusations, and then make sure none of those charges applies to you.

Self-Check

1. On a scale of 1–10, with 10 being highest, how would you rate your work ethic?

   _____

   What do others think about your ability to see a project through with quality and productivity?

   _____

2. What instances lately show you have learned to put your own pleasure behind other goals?

   _____

   _____

3. Describe your idea of commitment and dedication. Give examples.

   _____

   _____

4. What can you do in your own life now to make all those accusations against your generation not true for you?

_____

_____

5. Give three examples that show you have moved beyond the bad raps your generation receives from employers and the adult world.

_____

_____

_____

_____

6. What adult quality do you feel you have developed to a high degree? Explain.

_____

_____

_____

Facing the Future 19

Planning Ahead without Losing Yours

No one has a crystal ball, and there are no classes in your school that guarantee things that will happen in the future.

One class many colleges don't offer, and one which would really be a worthwhile addition to any curriculum, is a course in which you could study the future. There are experts who make predictions, and certain trends can give clues, but no one will ever be able to prepare perfectly for what lies ahead. As we have said earlier, the one best way to prepare for the future is to be well grounded in the basics of your chosen career. Then learn to be comfortable with change. Doing that, you can be fairly sure you'll be able to cope, survive, and even succeed with whatever comes.

No Small Change

Learn to deal with change. The one fact you can accept with absolute certainty is that you, your entire life, and the world around you are all on the move, and movement involves change.

Change does not have much respect for whatever is. It is more concerned with what will be and what can be. You can save yourself a lot of frustration throughout your life if you can accept the fact that change will occur and that often, when you have gotten familiar with things as they have become, they'll turn around and become something else! That drives some people crazy. It drives others to greatness.

The best way for you to respond successfully to life's challenges will be to have some solid knowledge of skills, abilities, and fundamentals behind you. Any job you enter will require a certain training period in specifics and particular requirements, but most prospective employers will presume you have a foundation of information upon which you can build.

Many of the classes you're taking now have no direct link to the career you may be pursuing fifteen years from now, but every lecture and every assignment is geared to giving you more background information, as well as helping you develop skills in research and analytical thinking. As much as you may often wonder about it, there is a method to the seeming madness of most college curricula. The more you know, the easier it will be to learn new things. Life even becomes more enjoyable and humorous once you have a broad background of facts and knowledge. You become more able to understand people's allusions and jokes!

Keep your options open. Don't set inflexible goals that allow only for all or nothing. If maturity teaches an individual anything, it teaches that very few things are all black or all white. Life is made up of many shades of grey. Don't make yourself willing to work in only one area of the country, and don't tell yourself you haven't succeeded if you don't land the exact, specific kind of job you have in mind. The same attitude should even help you find a compatible marriage partner.

There is a lot of growing still ahead of you, so don't presume anything. There are some people who leave college with the attitude that the world is going to hand its best to them on that proverbial silver platter. These people can get very fussy with job offers and salaries, and once they do secure a position, they are often unhappy when they learn they have to start at the bottom and work their way up. They have to pay some dues.

Pay Your Dues   A realistic attitude toward the future should include an acceptance on your part that you may have to work for a little less at first, and possibly do some less-important jobs on your way to the top rungs of any organization. On the other hand, don't let yourself presume that everyone in the business world, as well as the world in general, is out to get you and use you.

Most personnel directors, commenting on college graduates who come for job interviews, cite attitude as one quality that is all-important. A college grad can come into an interview with an impressive transcript and even perhaps a few honors and accomplishments to his or her credit. However, that person has not had any classes in attitude. This is something that has evolved and that stems directly from the individual's personality.

Personnel representatives know that the job-seeker has a certain amount of brains and wants to work. They also know that the prospective employee can be taught additional skills as they are needed at various performance levels. The one intangible personnel directors look for is the state of an individual's attitude.

Is this young person positive and motivated? Will he or she be the type to join in a team effort, or is there a certain amount of negativism that labels him or her as one of the cynics of the company's future? The answers to those questions often determine whether or not that person is hired.

A lot of young people are afraid to go into job interviews with confidence. True, they have minimal working experience behind them, but a positive attitude and firm belief in their own abilities to learn and eventually succeed often can make the difference between getting or losing a job.

Don't prepare to leave college with the feeling that you will have to claw your way up every rung of the corporate ladder or fight your way through life. It won't help your attitude, and it won't help your ability to relate openly with people. Such a feeling also may set you off as a person who expects nothing and who, because of that, someday will be satisfied with nothing.

As you near the end of your college career, take the time to attend any workshops offered on developing a resume. Most college placement bureaus will help you, and you are wise to take advantage of this service. Then, when you feel you have written a good resume, spend a little well-placed money and invest in having a professional service develop a unique, tailor-made resume for you. It makes a big difference and shows you understand the ground rules of breaking into the business world.

Presume Away! There are certain things you can presume about the future, along with the fact it will change. Go ahead and presume all you want that there will be people in and out of your life who will love you and honestly care what happens to you.

Presume that your positive attitude and fair amount of realistic aggressiveness will set you apart from the majority who simply muddle through life, wallowing in their own mediocrity, letting others push them around, and settling for what society or authority figures determine is best for them. The gently aggressive and confident prospective employee is always a pleasure to interview. Any positive, realistic, and aware person is always looked upon as a potential good employee and is somehow assured of a place in the forefront of society's future accomplishments.

Welcome the future; don't fear it. Accept it as a lively and challenging friend, not as an enemy with whom you must constantly fight and struggle. The world out there isn't waiting to see your degrees and awards. It is waiting to see your ability to deal with others, to challenge yourself, and to motivate yourself toward whatever goals you set. Some of those goals will concern your career. Others will deal with your own personal life, your needs, and your desires to feel good about yourself.

Most people have never learned how to channel their energies and practice the delicate art of self-direction. Because of this, the true leaders, the initiators, the innovators, and the succeeders come from the ranks of those few who have learned to look the future in the eye and refuse to accept defeat. They come from that group of people who understand, but who also continue to learn, who have confidence and creativity, but who are also willing to listen to others. The true success is the person who continues to learn, and never turns away from the challenges life demands, or which come from within his or her own self.

Be Prepared The Scouts have a good idea. It helps to be prepared.

As you look toward the years ahead, it may be good to realize that success will not come quickly or automatically. Since you have little or no experience in a profession, you'll have to start near the bottom. You may even have to do some experimenting with a few jobs before you find one that is a comfortable challenge and suited to your talents and psychological disposition.

As you mature even more, you'll have to assess your ability to deal with people. With most of your youth behind you, it would be wise to check your communication skills and your talent for dealing confidently with others. You'll need to begin asserting yourself more. Be ready to speak intelligently in many different kinds of situations. If you still feel lacking in this regard, take a public speaking class as an elective, or attend seminars on interviewing as well as effective communication.

Realize that there may be a certain amount of jealousy in some of your future co-workers. They may have not gone to college and, relying on the experience of their years, may resent your diploma and your new methods. You may find people who are jealous of your youth and the opportunities that lie ahead of you. You'll find others who seem congenial and helpful at first but who are simply trying to relive their own youth through you.

One of the best ways you can equip yourself for the future is to think back through all your years of living and comprehend what has happened to you so far. This will give you the beginning of wisdom. You don't have all the answers, but promise yourself that there will be no one in the world more willing to try to find them. Accept the fact that you don't know everything, and maintain a constant willingness to learn. Remember those people who seem to constantly argue for their own mediocrity? Don't fall into that trap. You know what you know. You are more knowledgeable and better than many people. Now you must face the real challenge—you must learn to be better than yourself!

The future can be a frightening and lonely place, but with a positive attitude and a sense of your own worth and ability, it can become one of the most exciting places of all. There is more progress being made today in areas including science, medicine, business, communication, and the humanities than ever before. This world is very much like you. It's still on its way and shows no sign of tiring or ending. All you have to do is decide to move with it!

It's easy to get mired in ruts of daily living and to forget the possibilities of success, achievement, and love that lie ahead of you. Don't forget them. Just remember and believe, as strongly as you have ever believed anything, that the best is yet to be.

Self-Check

1. Are you more depressed or more optimistic about your future? Detail your answer.

_____

_____

2. What are your plans for the immediate time after college, and how do these fit into your career goals?

_____

_____

3. What have you learned from your more serious mistakes over the past two years? Explain.

_____

4. On a scale of 1–10, with 10 being the highest, rate your realistic chances for a happy, successful life. Give reasons for your answer.

_____

_____

_____

5. Do you feel any cynicism about your chances for securing a good job or having a good marriage?

_____

Why do you feel this way? _____

_____

6. Rate your attitude in relation to its positiveness and energy.

_____

_____

7. What specific changes can you make during the next year to improve your attitude and optimism?

_____

_____

_____

You Bet
Your Life

And You Win!   Your college diploma is costing a great deal of money. How much you've had to work for that money matters. What matters most, though, is how hard you can learn to work while you are in college. That will set the foundation and the groundwork you are laying for the rest of your life. How successful you are at this time gives a good indication of your performance ahead.

Be an Initiator   Take a few tips to heart. First, gear yourself toward success. Don't be a responder; be an initiator. There are many people who seem to wait for life to happen to them, for things to happen to them; then they respond. While life will always throw you many curves, your ability to respond well will come from how often you initiate what happens to and for you.

Make at least part of your life happen for you. Keep a journal or a calendar book, then use it to set goals and arrange times for things to happen. Set the wheels turning for yourself. When you have had an event in your life happen, deal with it, mourn whatever loss it has caused you or celebrate its joy, and try to gain some perspective on it. Then grab hold of the reins of your own life again and plan the steps ahead.

Second, make an effort to get people who count into your life. As your own support group, they can help you keep believing in yourself. Many young people, thinking they need full social lives, spend a lot of valuable time with others they know won't be future friends. They sell themselves out doing things and believing things that really aren't part of their nature.

Don't waste time cultivating weeds. Find positive people who believe in you. They will blossom into real friends as the years move on.

Third, keep alive a strong belief in your own self-worth. We all have failures, bad days, and times when we are down. Don't let depression dig its claws into you, though, and don't allow long periods of "down time" in your life. The world is crying out for strong people who can make a difference. If you can keep your head on straight and your attitude positive, you are a great asset to the world you know and to the world that waits to meet you.

Remember when we said joy needs energy? So does a positive approach. Get the sleep you need, at least once in a while, and take care of your body enough to keep physical energy strong. Keeping belief in yourself and your ability to make a difference on the planet will keep you psychologically strong, too.

By being an initiator in your life, keeping good people around you, and staying positive, you will set a strong new tone for the years ahead. That tone will keep you positive and build the feeling that you are in control. You are on top of your life; it isn't running you.

The Big Question

Are these four years of study—stretching your mind, coping with new challenges, spending a great deal of money, and reaching for new goals—worth it?

You have given up a lot of your life and a lot of your own preferences to be where you are now. If you're at all honest with yourself, there will be times then you wonder if the effort you put into college work is well placed. It is.

Every day when education is your main task is a precious time. Anything that takes concentration and effort should have some degree of worthiness in the plan of your life.

Take Charge

Most people presume that, once you are in college, you have set some distinct goals for yourself, and you can see a reason for all the hard work and self-sacrifice you are asked to make. And you know now that the only way to succeed in your college years and in your life is to move beyond the stereotypes. Be your own person, set realistic goals, and take charge of your life in a positive way. If you can understand the value of what you're doing and realize the good it can cause in a ripple effect throughout the rest of your life, that hard work and those long hours you are spending now can become extremely meaningful.

Many young people drift through their early years, never establishing priorities and values. They're too busy living from day to day, and after all, they reason, they still have time for those "heavier" things later on. College, however, is the perfect place where you can decide what is really important and worth extra effort. College is worth it. These years are not only worth your effort and someone's money. They are a real bargain!

What should you bring to college, even if you have only a few more months before your graduation? Try an honest attempt to get along with others, a good degree of self-motivation, a healthy amount of ambitious willingness to work and to achieve, determination, and above all, faith in yourself!

College is worth it because you are worth it. It's that simple!

People Need People

One of the most important aspects of your life now, as always, is the people with whom you spend your time. Much of your attitude toward school and the whole process of learning can be made more optimistic and productive if you can find people who share your values.

Even if it takes more time and you have to look a little harder, don't stop trying to find those who are not worried about image as much as they are about ideas. Find the people who are confident enough in themselves to care about someone and something else. And when you find these good friends, keep them as a precious part of your life.

They can make hard times much easier to take. When you need encouragement, they'll be there, not necessarily agreeing with you, but helping you keep your perspective and priorities on the right track.

If it's true that love makes the world go around, remember it is people who love, in many different kinds of ways. Your years in college give you a real opportunity to meet and get to know new people who are not afraid to share, understand, and dream a few dreams. Don't let that opportunity go to waste.

The Right to Succeed

Channeling your energies in the right directions will also help. You begin by understanding that a few actions will be required of you if you're going to feel the success you need to help you proceed through these college years. You know you'll have to talk, especially in discussion classes, as well as around your dorm and in places where others congregate. College is definitely not the place to set up a hermitlike existence. That not only keeps others away and sets you off in isolation, it also keeps you from learning and experiencing many good things.

You say you have a tendency to be shy? You also have a right to succeed! If reaching out toward others takes more effort than you would like to expend right now, look at the results you can achieve and give the effort to make contact.

Another thing you'll be expected to do is search. Allowing yourself to be educated—and yes, it does take your will to allow that phenomenon to happen—presumes you know there are matters you still do not totally understand. Allow yourself to reach and to try, and with that open mind you intend to carry with you the rest of your life, check into seminars and personal development courses. They may be in areas such as leadership, problem solving, or other psychologically helpful topics. Use them. Even if you don't know exactly what you intend to gain from them, sign up, presuming you will grow. And you know what? You will.

Rapping It Up

College is expensive, all right, and the expense comes in many areas besides financial. You and your parents are making a lot of sacrifices to pay the bills. You, if you have the right perspective, are spending much more in effort, self-discipline, and personal commitment.

You can succeed in college very well, just as you can succeed in life very well. Just keep your eye on some realistic goals as you travel, and promise yourself you won't stop trying. As you stand here on the threshold of adulthood and feel your life pulling you forward into an exciting and optimistic future, look back at the efforts you've made in the past and acknowledge with great joy some of your earlier victories. Any time you are involved in a difficult situation that takes a long time, it is normal to get bogged down in details and lose sight of the complete goal.

Don't let that happen to you in regard to your education. You are learning from books, and you are learning from people. Most of all, you are learning from life itself as it constantly hands you new experiences and challenges that may, at first, seem strange and totally out of your league.

You can survive college by squeaking through in your classes. Where college becomes a real success story and worth all the effort, though, is in your own growth as a person. If someday you can walk away from school more confident in yourself and your talents, secure in your ability to deal with others, and realizing that you will always be learning and encountering new opportunities for growth and a deepening of your awareness, then your college experience will be a roaring success.

Any effort you make to improve your mind and attain your goals is worth it. Although you may not change the world, you will have a definite impact on the lives of those around you—not only by being educated, but also by being truly knowledgeable, sensitive, and aware as you take your place in this larger arena of education they call life.

You know there is always help available. You know there are people who love you and, by now, you should know that your greatest source of energy and success, in college and in life, lies within you. It lies in your will and in your ability to assert yourself, to understand your own strengths and weaknesses, and to continue to move on, always learning and always growing.

Self-Check   1. How do you spend your free time? How are those activities preparing you for your future?

_____

_____

2. Define two goals that are keeping you in college now.

_____

_____

_____

3. On a scale of 1–10, with 10 being the highest, how would you rate your self-direction and self-motivation?

_____

Name two ways you could improve it in two specific areas.

_____

_____

4. Name three things that are keeping you from greater success in class and in your decision-making capabilities.

_____

_____

_____

5. When you drive away from your campus for the last time, what do you think will be your fondest memories, your deepest regrets, and your greatest successes?

_____

_____

_____

_____

6. What do you feel will have contributed most to your growth as a person at the end of these college years?

_____

_____

7. End this book with three reasons why you are a success already, in your life and in your schooling so far.

    _____

    _____

    _____

    _____

Be Good to Yourself!

VGM CAREER BOOKS

OPPORTUNITIES IN
Available in both paperback and hardbound editions
Accounting
Acting
Advertising
Aerospace
Agriculture
Airline
Animal and Pet Care
Architecture
Automotive Service
Banking
Beauty Culture
Biological Sciences
Biotechnology
Book Publishing
Broadcasting
Building Construction Trades
Business Communication
Business Management
Cable Television
Carpentry
Chemical Engineering
Chemistry
Child Care
Chiropractic Health Care
Civil Engineering
Cleaning Service
Commercial Art and Graphic Design
Computer Aided Design and
    Computer Aided Mfg.
Computer Maintenance
Computer Science
Counseling & Development
Crafts
Culinary
Customer Service
Dance
Data Processing
Dental Care
Direct Marketing
Drafting
Electrical Trades
Electronic and Electrical Engineering
Electronics
Energy
Engineering
Engineering Technology
Environmental
Eye Care
Fashion
Fast Food
Federal Government
Film
Financial
Fire Protection Services
Fitness
Food Services
Foreign. Language
Forestry
Gerontology
Government Service
Graphic Communications
Health and Medical
High Tech
Home Economics
Hospital Administration
Hotel & Motel Management
Human Resources Management
    Careers
Information Systems
Insurance
Interior Design
International Business
Journalism
Laser Technology
Law

Law Enforcement and Criminal Justice
Library and Information Science
Machine Trades
Magazine Publishing
Management
Marine & Maritime
Marketing
Materials Science
Mechanical Engineering
Medical Technology
Metalworking
Microelectronics
Military
Modeling
Music
Newspaper Publishing
Nursing
Nutrition
Occupational Therapy
Office Occupations
Opticiany
Optometry
Packaging Science
Paralegal Careers
Paramedical Careers
Part-time & Summer Jobs
Performing Arts
Petroleum
Pharmacy
Photography
Physical Therapy
Physician
Plastics
Plumbing & Pipe Fitting
Podiatric Medicine
Postal Service
Printing
Property Management
Psychiatry
Psychology
Public Health
Public Relations
Purchasing
Real Estate
Recreation and Leisure
Refrigeration and Air Conditioning
Religious Service
Restaurant
Retailing
Robotics
Sales
Sales & Marketing
Secretarial
Securities
Social Science
Social Work
Speech-Language Pathology
Sports & Athletics
Sports Medicine
State and Local Government
Teaching
Technical Communications
Telecommunications
Television and Video
Theatrical Design & Production
Transportation
Travel
Trucking
Veterinary Medicine
Visual Arts
Vocational and Technical
Warehousing
Waste Management
Welding
Word Processing
Writing
Your Own Service Business

CAREERS IN
Accounting; Advertising;
Business; Communications; Computers;
Education; Engineering; Health Care;
High Tech; Law; Marketing; Medicine;
Science

CAREER DIRECTORIES
Careers Encyclopedia
Dictionary of Occupational Titles
Occupational Outlook Handbook

CAREER PLANNING
Admissions Guide to Selective
    Business Schools
Career Planning and Development for
    College Students and Recent
    Graduates
Careers Checklists
Careers for Animal Lovers
Careers for Bookworms
Careers for Culture Lovers
Careers for Foreign Language
    Aficionados
Careers for Good Samaritans
Careers for Gourmets
Careers for Nature Lovers
Careers for Numbers Crunchers
Careers for Sports Nuts
Careers for Travel Buffs
Guide to Basic Resume Writing
Handbook of Business and
    Management Careers
Handbook of Health Care Careers
Handbook of Scientific and
    Technical Careers
How to Change Your Career
How to Choose the Right Career
How to Get and Keep
    Your First Job
How to Get into the Right Law School
How to Get People to Do Things
    Your Way
How to Have a Winning Job Interview
How to Land a Better Job
How to Make the Right Career Moves
How to Market Your College Degree
How to Prepare a *Curriculum Vitae*
How to Prepare for College
How to Run Your Own Home Business
How to Succeed in Collge
How to Succeed in High School
How to Write a Winning Resume
Joyce Lain Kennedy's Career Book
Planning Your Career of Tomorrow
Planning Your College Education
Planning Your Military Career
Planning Your Young Child's
    Education
Resumes for Advertising Careers
Resumes for College Students & Recent
    Graduates
Resumes for Communications Careers
Resumes for Education Careers
Resumes for High School Graduates
Resumes for High Tech Careers
Resumes for Sales and Marketing Careers
Successful Interviewing for College
    Seniors

SURVIVAL GUIDES
Dropping Out or Hanging In
High School Survival Guide
College Survival Guide

VGM Career Horizons
a division of *NTC Publishing Group*
4255 West Touhy Avenue
Lincolnwood, Illinois 60646-1975